The Mikado

W9-COX-663

or

THE TOWN OF TITIPU

Book by

W.S. Gilbert

Music by

Arthur Sullivan

Authentic Version Edited by

Bryceson Treharne

This score includes all the dialogue.

Orchestral material is available on rental from G. Schirmer, Inc.

P.O. Box 572
445 Bellvale Road
Chester, NY 10918
(845) 469-2271
(845) 469-7544 (fax)
www.schirmer.com

Ed. 1624

ISBN 0-88188-724-2

Copyright © 2002 by G. Schirmer, Inc. (ASCAP), New York, NY
International Copyright Secured. All Rights Reserved.
Warning: Unauthorized reproduction of this publication is prohibited by Federal Law and subject to criminal prosecution.

G. SCHIRMER, *Inc.*

DISTRIBUTED BY

HAL•LEONARD® CORPORATION

7777 W. BLUEMOUND RD. P.O. BOX 13819 MILWAUKEE, WI 53213

DRAMATIS PERSONAE

The Mikado of Japan

Nanki-Poo ....*His Son, disguised as a wandering minstrel, and in love with Yum-Yum*

Ko-Ko ....*Lord High Executioner of Titipu*

Pooh-Bah ....*Lord High Everything Else*

Pish-Tush ....*A Noble Lord*

Yum-Yum ....
Pitti-Sing .... } ....*Three Sisters, Wards of Ko-Ko*
Peep-Bo............................

Katisha...*An Elderly Lady, in love with Nanki-Poo*

Chorus of School-Girls, Nobles, Guards, and Coolies

ACT I—Courtyard of Ko-Ko's Official Residence

ACT II—Ko-Ko's Garden

MUSICAL NUMBERS

ARGUMENT

Before the action of the opera begins, Nanki-Poo has fled from the court of his father, the Mikado of Japan, to escape marriage with an elderly lady, named Katisha. Assuming the disguise of a musician, he has then fallen in love with a fair maiden, Yum-Yum; but he has been prevented from marrying her by her guardian, Ko-Ko, who wishes to marry her himself. Ko-Ko, however, has been condemned to death for flirting. When Act I opens, Nanki-Poo is hastening to the court of Ko-Ko in Titipu to find out whether Yum-Yum is now free to marry him.

From Pooh-Bah (a corrupt and proud public official) and Pish-Tush (a nobleman), Nanki-Poo learns that Ko-Ko has, instead, become Lord High Executioner, thus preventing the sentence of decapitation from being carried out. Ko-Ko is, in fact, going to marry Yum-Yum that very afternoon.

Everything seems to be going well for Ko-Ko, but suddenly a letter comes from the Mikado ordering him to execute somebody or else lose his position of Lord High Executioner. He is in a quandary to find someone to execute, when Nanki-Poo appears, bent upon suicide because he cannot marry Yum-Yum. By conceding to him the right to marry Yum-Yum for a month, Ko-Ko persuades Nanki-Poo to be the subject for the public execution when that month is up. There is general rejoicing in this apparent solution to the problem, marred only by the unexpected appearance of Katisha, in quest of the vanished object of her affections, Nanki-Poo. She is driven away, but threatens to go to the Mikado about the matter.

Act II opens with Yum-Yum preparing for her marriage with Nanki-Poo. As all are singing a "merry madrigal," Ko-Ko comes in with the news that he has just discovered a law stating that when a married man is executed, his wife must be buried alive. To save Yum-Yum from that fate, Nanki-Poo decides to kill himself at once. But this again throws Ko-Ko into a quandary to find someone to execute (especially as he has heard that the Mikado is at that moment on his way to Titipu). Nanki-Poo magnanimously offers himself for immediate decapitation, but Ko-Ko is unable to perform the act without some practice.

Another way out of the difficulty presents itself: Ko-Ko has Pooh-Bah make a false affidavit that Nanki-Poo has been executed, and bids Nanki-Poo and Yum-Yum leave the country.

The Mikado soon appears. Ko-Ko thinks that the object of this visit is to see whether the execution has taken place. He accordingly produces the affidavit and describes with gusto the execution. But the Mikado has actually come at the prompting of Katisha in search of his lost son. When the fact transpires that the person whom Ko-Ko has supposedly executed is really the Mikado's son, Ko-Ko and his accomplices are declared guilty of "compassing the death of the Heir Apparent." The only hope for them is to admit the falsehood of the affidavit and produce Nanki-Poo alive. But, as Nanki-Poo has already married Yum-Yum and so cannot marry Katisha, Katisha will surely insist on the execution of Nanki-Poo and Yum-Yum. Ko-Ko solves the problem by offering his hand to Katisha; and, after he sings her the touching ballad of "Willow, tit-willow," she accepts him. The end of the opera comes with Nanki-Poo's discovering himself as the son of the Mikado.

GILBERT & SULLIVAN

W.S. Gilbert

Arthur Sullivan

THE GILBERT & SULLIVAN PARTNERSHIP

By Marie Eggold

In fourteen operettas over the course of twenty-five years, W.S. Gilbert and Arthur Sullivan etched their names in the history books forever. Their works not only created an English school of light opera, they whetted an appetite for musical theater in the United States and around the world. Their works have inspired a steady stream of recordings, revivals, books, and articles over the past century, with films and web sites appearing more recently. Gilbert and Sullivan have remained at the heart of the operetta repertoire for more than 100 years. Yet for Gilbert, who aspired to write serious dramas, and Sullivan, who aspired to write serious music, writing entertainment for the Victorian middle class was not quite fulfilling.

Although one seldom hears the names Gilbert and Sullivan spoken separately, the two had careers independent of one another. They were also remarkably different men. Gilbert was well over six feet tall and fair complected, with a rather grim face. Sullivan on the other hand was quite short, dark haired, and was known for an easy smile and twinkling eyes. As Gilbert aged, he retained a youthful vigor that allowed him to show off occasional dance steps in his later years, just to prove that he still could. Sullivan's health was poor. He was stricken with a painful kidney ailment and walked with a cane while still a young man. Gilbert was regarded as one of the most prominent dramatists of his day, while Sullivan was seen as someone with a tremendous gift that he failed to develop fully.

William Schwenck Gilbert

William Schwenck Gilbert was born on November 18, 1836, just a few months before the reign of Queen Victoria began. His father, Dr. William Gilbert, had served as a naval surgeon until an inheritance allowed him to retire to travel and write. In later years the younger Gilbert, called Schwenck by his family, would illustrate some of his father's publications. Schwenck studied law and practiced briefly, but soon turned his attention to writing. He was a frequent contributor to *Fun* magazine, publishing drawings, short stories, and dramatic criticism. Best remembered of his work from this time are the *Bab Ballads*, stories in verse that he signed with his childhood nickname. The name is short for "Babby," his family's twist on baby.

Topics and ideas from the *Bab Ballads* and other early works show up, fleshed out, in the operettas, as do several recurring themes. The Gilbert family often told the story of how Schwenck had been kidnapped while they were in Italy. He was only missing for a few hours, quickly returned for a small bit of money. But he claimed to have a memory of the event, likely just familiarity from hearing the tale repeated throughout his childhood. The idea of two children switched at birth, and the ensuing crisis of identity and social class, pops up again and again in his works, most notably in *The Pirates of Penzance*. Another theme was one of topsy-turvy worlds. Gilbert was fascinated by plots and scenarios based on things being just the opposite of what they should be. Virtue was evil, peace was war, etc. He explored the idea in his one-act extravaganza, *Topsyturveydom*, which opened on March 21, 1874, returning to it throughout his career. By the mid-1870s, Gilbert was well-known as a playwright.

From the first "official" biography of Gilbert, which appeared in 1923, to the 1935 Hesketh Pearson book *Gilbert and Sullivan*, and his 1957 *Gilbert–His Life and Strife*, William Schwenck Gilbert was painted as a kindly, fairly typical British gentleman. In fact, Gilbert was a very difficult man. "I am an ill-tempered pig," he once wrote, "and I glory in it." In the book *Between Ourselves* (1930), Seymour Hicks wrote of Gilbert, "He always gave me the impression that he got up in the morning to see with whom he could have a quarrel." Indeed, Gilbert seemed to relish quarrels. He was an extremely litigious man. He saw personal slights at every turn and was not content until things were put right, in his favor of course. His stock line in such situations was, "I shall place the matter at once in the hands of my solicitor."

Arthur Sullivan

Arthur Sullivan, on the other hand, was a kind, likeable man with no great ego. He enjoyed having fun and was somewhat notorious for his various appetites, which included incessant travel, encounters with prostitutes, and constant indulging in fine foods and wines. He was born on May 13, 1842, to a bandmaster who filled his son's life with music and recognized the boy's talents early. By 1856, Arthur was a scholarship student at the Royal Academy of Music, studying at the Leipzig Conservatory from 1858 to 1861. His instructors there believed he had a greater musical gift than Brahms. Later it was said that he had greater ability than any English musician since Purcell. In the face of such lavish praise, his work in operettas, no matter how popular and successful they might be, was viewed by critics as a waste of a tremendous talent.

A conductor, educator, and organist, in addition to being a composer, Sullivan had written a good deal of "serious" music by the time he began his partnership with Gilbert. He always viewed his theater work as secondary to serious composition, which included choral works, a symphony, a ballet, and numerous hymns, the most famous being "Onward Christian Soldiers." Yet an article that appeared in the *Pall Mall Gazette* at the time of the premiere of *The Gondoliers* declared Sullivan England's most popular composer—popularity won by operettas. The same biographers who overlooked Gilbert's irascible nature treated Sullivan's easy-going personality and voracious appetites harshly.

The recipient of several honorary doctorates, Sullivan was not an intellectual, nor was he a literary man. He was, however, remembered by colleagues as a remarkable wit. Perhaps his greatest musical gift was his uncanny ability to contrive music to fit any lyric, any scene, and any mood. His music became an integral part of the theatrical scene, not a separate element. He would tailor his melodies to Gilbert's pattering poetry, gild a tune to match the sets or dances of a particular scene, and orchestrate the entire thing with grace and good humor.

The Partnership

The Gilbert and Sullivan partnership was actually a trio. The third partner was Richard D'Oyly Carte, who served as the catalyst who made the creative pair household names. Carte was the son of Richard Carte, a flautist and partner in the musical instrument manufacturing firm of Rudall, Carte and Co. He started out in his father's business, wrote some operettas, and conducted as well. But by the time he was twenty-five, he had set up his own theatrical and concert agency. Carte was not involved in Gilbert and Sullivan's first collaboration, *Thespis, or The Gods Grown Old*, which opened at the Gaiety Theatre on December 26, 1871. The libretto and score were never published and all but two numbers have been lost. Carte brought the writers together for *Trial By Jury*, which opened at the Royalty Theatre on March 25, 1875, performed with two other pieces. It outlived the productions with which it shared a bill and set Carte in motion. He interested several investing partners, leased the Opera Comique and announced the creation of the Comedy Opera Company. The company produced *The Sorcerer*, which opened on October 17, 1877, and *HMS Pinafore*, which opened on May 25, 1878. Although *Pinafore* had opened to receptive audiences and positive reviews, an unusually hot summer kept people out of the theaters and began a rift between Carte and the investors that eventually led to their separation. This left Carte free to form a partnership with the librettist and composer. The company was first known as Mr. D'Oyly Carte's Company until the name was changed in 1889 to The D'Oyly Carte Opera Company. With Carte at the helm, Gilbert and Sullivan created *The Pirates of Penzance*, which opened in England on December 30, 1879 and in New York a day later. *Patience* followed, opening in London on April 23, 1881.

Carte then built the Savoy Theatre in London, devoted to the production of the work of Gilbert and Sullivan. Erected on the site of the palace of Savoy that had been destroyed in the late 1300s, it was a strikingly modern theater. In fact, it was the world's first theater to be completely lit by electricity. With electricity came the ability to create lighting effects, which helped draw audiences to productions. A generator located in an empty lot beside the theater provided the power. A few years later Carte opened the Savoy Hotel on that lot, which was also a progressive building at the time. The Savoy Theatre hosted the premieres of *Iolanthe* in 1882, *Princess Ida* in 1884, *The Mikado* in 1885, *Ruddigore* in 1887, *The Yeoman of the Guard* in 1888, *The Gondoliers* in 1889, *Utopia Limited* in 1893, and *The Grand Duke* in 1896.

The Ocean Was Not Always Blue

Despite the levity of the operettas, the partnership was not bliss. Carte was building a new theater, the Royal English Opera House, in which he intended to premiere Sullivan's grand opera, *Ivanhoe*. Although the January 31, 1891 premiere was received with accolades, the public was not ready to embrace grand opera as it had embraced light opera. Carte eventually sold the theater. Meanwhile, as *Ruddigore* was running and Sullivan was preparing *Ivanhoe*, Gilbert took a close look at the accounts for the partnership. He found an expense of £140 to re-carpet the Savoy lobby and took offense. He felt that he and Sullivan should not be charged for such an extravagance. Sullivan sided with Carte. What ensued, remembered as the famous "Carpet Quarrel," created a wound that would not heal. The partnership was dissolved. Eventually the trio put their differences aside and created *Utopia Limited* and *The Grand Duke*, but things were never the same. Even in the best of times, Gilbert and Sullivan referred to each other by their surnames. Gilbert was constantly at war with one or another cast member, making rehearsals awkward affairs by giving his undivided attention to everyone but the party at whom he was angry. When the offending actor did a scene, Gilbert would pointedly ignore the goings-on, turning his back to the stage and making a great show of talking to someone until the scene was over.

Following *The Gondoliers*, the Savoy was largely devoted to revivals of Gilbert and Sullivan's operettas, or to pieces written by Sullivan with another librettist. But the partnership Gilbert/Sullivan/D'Oyly Carte would not have survived the 1890s regardless of the "Carpet Quarrel." Both Sullivan and Carte were in failing health. Sullivan's health had been in a long decline, his kidney disease causing him horrendous pain. He died on November 22, 1900. Carte survived him by just six months. Gilbert however, maintained a vigorous lifestyle to the end. On May 29, 1911 the seventy-four-year-old Gilbert endeavored to teach two women to swim in the lake he had created at his home. When one of the women floundered, Gilbert dove in to save her, suffering a fatal heart attack in the water.

The Legacy

The magic of the Gilbert and Sullivan partnership lay in the cutting wit and perfectionism of Gilbert, who micro-managed details of rehearsals, and his ability to craft a plot of many convoluted layers, only to have it all sort out neatly in the end. Along the way he would poke fun at social conventions, the law, and romance. Sullivan was the one who made froth of this wit. He could craft melodies that instantly projected the dramatic intent of Gilbert's lines. He was fearless in his treatment of rhythms. He rose to such challenges as setting the mouthfuls of lyrics presented by "I am the Very Model of a Modern Major General," creating an operetta classic. Their contributions did not go unrecognized. Sullivan was knighted in 1883. Gilbert was knighted in 1907.

The D'Oyly Carte Opera Company continued presenting and touring the works of Gilbert and Sullivan until financial difficulties forced it to close in 1982. The D'Oyly Carte Opera Trust had been formed in 1961, when the copyrights ran out on the operettas. In her will, Dame Bridget Carte left £1 million to the trust, earmarking it to reform the company. The company reappeared in 1988, returning to the Savoy Theatre in 2000.

THE MIKADO

By Marie Eggold

Gilbert and Sullivan's most successful and most popular operetta, *The Mikado, or The Town of Titipu*, grew from quarrel between its creators. W.S. Gilbert and Arthur Sullivan were never close friends. Most of their communication was through letters, though they lived near one another, or through producer Richard D'Oyly Carte, the glue that held the partnership together.

Sullivan was viewed as England's greatest hope for an internationally respected serious composer, a perceived potential not quite fitting with the frothy music of operettas. Things rather came to a head when he was knighted in 1883. The knighthood itself might not have made a difference, but comments in the press certainly did. The *Musical Review* printed, "Some things that Mr. Arthur Sullivan may do, Sir Arthur Sullivan ought not to do." Sir George Grove, of *Grove's Dictionary of Music and Musicians* fame, commented, "Surely the time has come when so able and experienced a master of voice, orchestra, and stage effect—master too of so much genuine sentiment—may apply his gifts to a serious opera on some subject of abiding human or natural interest." Sullivan was listening. By the time *Princess Ida* opened at the Savoy Theatre on January 5, 1884, he was chafing in his role as a composer of comic operas. Three weeks after the premiere and its disappointing reception, Sullivan informed Carte that he did not intend to write any more Savoy light operas.

Carte assumed that, after a taking vacation, Sullivan would reconsider and take up the pen again. Gilbert apparently did as well, as he began work on another variation of his infamous "lozenge plot," the epitome of Gilbertian topsy-turviness, resurfacing year after year in one form or another. In the scheme, characters are transformed by consuming a magical lozenge, thereby gaining characteristics the opposite of their own natures: a shy person becomes outgoing, a good person becomes evil, and so on. Sullivan wanted nothing to do with the lozenge plot in any of its various incarnations, and was running out of patience with topsy-turviness in general. He headed for the Continent to recover from another attack of a chronic kidney disease. Carte wrote to Sullivan, explaining that the revenues from *Princess Ida* were dropping, and that a new opera would be needed soon. In accordance with the contract that Gilbert, Sullivan, and Carte had signed a year earlier, the creative team was required to produce a new operetta as needed on six months notice. Sullivan replied, "...it is impossible for me to do another piece of the character of those already written by Gilbert and myself."

When Sullivan returned to London, Gilbert came calling with a new version of the lozenge plot in hand. Sullivan rejected it outright. The letters exchanged reveal the depth of the chasm between the two men. Sullivan refused to write anything so "improbable" or "artificial." Gilbert responded by accusing Sullivan of being "arbitrary and capricious." Meanwhile, *Princess Ida* was running out of steam and there was no new opera to take the Savoy stage. Carte began running from Gilbert to Sullivan and back again, trying to mediate the dispute. Gilbert suggested that perhaps Sullivan might be happier working with another librettist. Sullivan said no, citing Gilbert's "matchless skill." Gilbert remained attached to the lozenge plot, but altered the libretto in hopes of bringing Sullivan to see its merits. In reply, the composer wrote, "I don't like the Lozenge, I stick to my objection." Gilbert wrote that considering the circumstance, he would not be able to write a libretto for the next opera. Sullivan responded by noting that Gilbert's statement was obviously final, stating, "I regret it very much."

At this point fact and legend become a bit blurred. The often-told story of Gilbert's inspiration for *The Mikado* places him in his study at Harrington Gardens, pacing furiously back and forth. Suddenly, a large Japanese ceremonial sword, decoratively hung on the wall, crashes to the floor. He told the story years later saying, "It suggested the broader idea." Perhaps. The story may have been a dramatic invention. London was in the grip of Japanese fever in 1884. No proper parlor was unadorned by Japanese ceramics or silks. An entire village had been set up at the Japanese Exhibition in Knightsbridge, with Japanese families going about their daily activities in something of a fish bowl for Londoners to examine and study. Gilbert would have been hard-pressed to miss the oriental mania around him. In fact, he found it quite silly.

Gilbert began sketching characters and costumes for a new comic opera set in Japan. He immediately wrote to Sullivan of the staging and costume opportunities offered by the oriental setting, as well the musical possibilities, adding that nothing like it had ever been attempted in England. Sullivan took the bait, with relief. "If I understand you to propose you will construct a plot without the supernatural and improbable elements, and on the lines which you describe," he wrote to Gilbert, "I gladly undertake to set it without further discussing the matter, or asking what the subject is to be." The rift was mended, although the handwriting was on the wall. It would be just a few years before the infamous "Carpet Quarrel" would forever damage the partnership. But for the moment, Gilbert and Sullivan were up and running again.

To fill the gap between *Princess Ida* and *The Mikado* on the Savoy stage, *The Sorcerer* and *Trial By Jury* were revived for the first time since their original productions at the Opera Comique. Gilbert enthusiastically delved into *The Mikado* preparations. He insisted from the outset that every detail be as authentic as possible. He ordered the best Japanese silk for costumes and engaged an authority in oriental art to help with designs. Most of the female principals in the show wore authentic garments; one costume was reputed to be over 200 years old. Gilbert ordered suits of Japanese military armor and mail, only to discover when they arrived that they were both too small and too heavy for his actors to wear. The sword from Gilbert's home, whether it inspired the operetta or not, indeed did appear in the original Savoy production.

Gilbert spotted three young women in the Savoy company, all equally short in stature, and was inspired by them to write "Three Little Maids from School." The ensemble has become emblematic of Gilbert and Sullivan, even for those who barely know their works. It was the first musical number Sullivan wrote when he began work on the score. "Three Little Maids" had to be repeated twice on opening night, in answer to thunderous applause.

Sullivan attacked the composition with his usual feverish pace, leaving the orchestration of the overture to someone else. The music is quintessentially British, with the exception of "Mi-ya sa-ma," which is an actual Japanese military march, complete with authentic words. Gilbert, the zealous auteur, had members of the Japanese Exhibition come to rehearsals to drill women in the cast in proper means of walking, bowing, and decorously hiding behind fans. The choreography and stage business of that original *Mikado* have remained a part of most productions for well over century. Gilbert honed and perfected the opera in rehearsals, nit-picking the cast at every turn and maintaining complete control over every detail. He badgered George Grossmith, who was playing Ko-Ko, until the actor was a nervous wreck, stumbling through parts of the opening performance in terror. Gilbert couldn't bear to watch the premiere, preferring to pace the city streets instead. However, he made sure to hear about it in great detail, and scheduled a rehearsal for the next morning to correct flaws in the performance.

The Mikado opened at the Savoy Theatre on March 14, 1885, to what one reviewer called a "tumultuous" reception. It ran at the Savoy for 672 uninterrupted performances, setting a record that would not be broken until 1922. Carte put a second company together immediately, ostensibly preparing them for a tour of England. But in truth, he had hired detectives to keep an eye on American pirate productions of the show. Carte's *Mikado* tour was secretly scheduled to open in New York at the Fifth Avenue Theatre in October. But a certain Mr. Duff was working on a pirate production set to open in that city in August. With international copyrights still woefully inadequate, Carte's only recourse was to open his own production first in New York, so that the pirate production would be a pale imitation of the original. When Duff sent someone to London to purchase Japanese silks at Liberty's department store, employees quickly grasped the situation and refused to sell to him. Duff's agent headed to Paris, but Carte was a step ahead of him, sending his own agent to buy up all the Japanese silk he could find first. Carte said, "I don't mind how much money I spend to smash Duff."

On learning via cable that Duff's production was indeed in rehearsals in New York, despite the attempted obstacles, Carte immediately went into high gear. The touring company was informed that it would not be touring the provinces as planned, but would instead be sailing across the Atlantic in secrecy. Company members were sworn to divulge nothing. Passage was booked on the Cunard line under assumed names. The cast, orchestra, and crews were forbidden to allow family see them off, and to avoid detection from fellow passengers were warned not to fraternize with one another onboard the ship. When the company arrived in New York, their secret still safe, Duff's posters were already up, announcing his opening of *The Mikado* in late August at the Standard Theatre. Although Duff managed to move his opening up a couple of days when he learned that Carte's company was in town, Carte trumped him. The D'Oyly Carte production of *The Mikado* opened in New York on August 19, 1885 to a wildly enthusiastic reception, eventually totalling an unprecedented run of 430 performances at the Fifth Avenue Theatre. Carte sent out several American touring companies, as well as British. Sullivan too traveled the US, as he had previously with *The Pirates of Penzance*, hailed as a genius wherever he went. Meanwhile, Gilbert stayed in London, torturing the Savoy company with incessant, fastidious rehearsals. He would creep about the theater during performances, finding fault wherever possible.

The popularity of *The Mikado* was astounding from the outset. On a particular evening in 1886, there were reported to be 170 different productions taking place in the United States. There was even a town in Michigan named after the operetta, and American society women created Japanese "Mikado rooms" in their homes. By the turn of the century the operetta had been translated into German, Hungarian, French, Russian, Swedish, Dutch, and Italian.

Strangely enough, *The Mikado*—once given a command performance for British royalty at Balmoral Castle—was temporarily banned in London by the British government during a state visit by Prince Fushimi of Japan. It was feared that the visiting dignitary might be offended by the Japanese caricatures. In fact, the operetta had already been presented in Japan by this time, under the title *Three Little Maids*. Japanese military bands also routinely played its music. After all, *The Mikado* is not a satire of Japanese culture, but rather a send-up of British law, social custom, and society. The Japanese trappings are merely a thin, exotic veil.

The Mikado has had various incarnations over the years. At the height of the operetta's popularity, Carte sent out a special performing company comprised entirely of children. Gilbert later wrote a children's book entitled *The Story of The Mikado*. A British version in the 1920s featured Katisha arriving in a car, the three maids clad in short skirts dancing a Charleston, and Yum-Yum bathing nude as Act II begins. In that same decade, an Oxford *Mikado* was costumed in modern dress. Two productions with African-American casts, *Swing Mikado* and *Hot Mikado*, played in New York concurrently in 1939. *Hot Mikado*, which reappears periodically, featured tap-dance-king Bill "Bojangles" Robinson. Groucho Marx appeared in a televised, abridged *Mikado* in the 1960s. London saw its own African-American *Mikado* in the 1970s. A new, large audience was gained with director Mike Leigh's 1999 film *Topsy-Turvy*, the story of Gilbert and Sullivan and the creation of *The Mikado*, featuring several extended excerpts.

THE MIKADO
Selected Discography

Recommended recordings:

1. The 1926 D'Oyly Carte recording, conducted by Harry Norris, first issued by RCA Victor in 1928; this is the first electrical recording of the opera (as opposed to the earlier acoustically recorded releases); reissued on LP and later on CD by Pearl; though the sound quality is poor, this is an important cast from the heyday of G&S singing. The Mikado: Darrell Fancourt; Nanki-Poo: Derek Oldham; Ko-Ko: Henry Lytton; Pooh-Bah: Leo Sheffield; Pish-Tush: George Baker; Go-To: T. Penry Hughes; Yum-Yum: Elsie Griffin; Pitti-Sing: Aileen Davies /Doris Hemingway /Beatrice Elburn; Peep-Bo Beatrice Elburn; Katisha: Bertha Lewis.

2. The 1936 D'Oyly Carte recording, conducted by Isidore Godfrey, released in 1936 by HMV, released by RCA Victor in 1937, issued on LP by RCA Victor in 1952, on LP by HMV in 1955, on LP by Arabesque in 1980 and 1982; issued on CD by Arabesque in 1986, by Pro Arte in 1992, by Happy Days in 1994, and on the 78s to CD label in 2001. The Mikado: Darrell Fancourt; Nanki-Poo: Derek Oldham; Ko-Ko: Martyn Green; Pooh-Bah: Sydney Granville; Pish-Tush: Leslie Rands; Go-To: L. Radley Flynn; Yum-Yum: Brenda Bennett; Pitti-Sing: Marjorie Eyre; Peep-Bo: Elizabeth Nickell-Lean; Katisha: Josephine Curtis; D'Oyly Carte Opera Chorus.

3. The 1936 D'Oyly Carte film soundtrack, conducted by Geoffrey Toye, issued in 1998 on CD on the Sounds on CD label (see also Filmography). The Mikado: John Barclay; Nanki-Poo: Kenny Baker; Pooh-Bah: Sydney Granville; Pish-Tush: Gregory Stroud; Yum-Yum: Jean Colin; Pitti-Sing: Elizabeth Paynter; Peep-Bo: Kathleen Naylor; Katisha: Constance Willis; D'Oyly Carte Opera Chorus.

4. The 1950 D'Oyly Carte recording, conducted by Isidore Godfrey, originally issued on both 78 and mono LP by Decca and London, reissued on stereo LP by Decca in 1979, on cassette by Price-Less in the 1980s, and on CD in 2001 by Sounds on CD, Pearl, Regis and Naxos. The Mikado: Darrell Fancourt; Nanki-Poo: Leonard Osborn; Ko-Ko: Martyn Green; Pooh-Bah: Richard Watson; Pish-Tush: Alan Styler; Go-To: L. Radley Flynn/Donald Harris; Yum-Yum: Margaret Mitchell; Pitti-Sing: Joan Gillingham; Peep-Bo: Joyce Wright; Katisha: Ella Halman; D'Oyly Carte Opera Chorus; New Promenade Orchestra.

5. The 1957 Glyndebourne recording, conducted by Sir Malcolm Sargent, originally issued on mono LP on HMV, on stereo LP on HMV in 1958, on Angel in the 1960s, on EMI on LP and cassette in 1976, digitally remastered for Angel/EMI in 1985 for LP and cassette then issued on CD in 1987, issued on CD by HMV in 1998, by EMI in 2001 as part of the complete Sargent Glyndebourne G&S recordings. The Mikado: Owen Brannigan; Nanki-Poo: Richard Lewis; Ko-Ko: Geraint Evans; Pooh-Bah: Ian Wallace; Pish-Tush: John Cameron; Yum-Yum: Elsie Morison; Pitti-Sing: Marjorie Thomas; Peep-Bo: Jeannette Sinclair; Katisha: Monica Sinclair; Glyndebourne Festival Chorus; Pro Arte Orchestra

6. The 1950 D'Oyly Carte recording, conducted by Isidore Godfrey, issued on LP 78 and LP in 1950 by Decca and London, on LP by Decca Ace of Clubs and Richmond in 1960, on CD in 2001 by Sounds on CD, Pearl, Regis and Naxos. The Mikado: Donald Adams; Nanki-Poo: Thomas Round; Ko-Ko: Peter Pratt; Pooh-Bah: Kenneth Sandford; Pish-Tush: Alan Styler; Go-To: Owen Grundy; Yum-Yum: Jean Hindmarsh; Pitti-Sing: Beryl Dixon; Peep-Bo: Jennifer Toye; Katisha: Ann Drummond-Grant; D'Oyly Carte Opera Chorus; New Symphony Orchestra of London.

7. The 1986 English National Opera recording, conducted by Peter Robinson, released on CD in 1986 by MCA and TER, by Musical Heritage Society in 1988, Koch International in 1994, as well as Showtime, Showstoppers and Jay in the late 1990s. The Mikado: Richard Angas; Nanki-Poo: Bonaventura Bottone; Ko-Ko: Eric Idle; Pooh-Bah: Richard Van Allan; Pish-Tush: Mark Richardson; Yum-Yum: Lesley Garrett; Pitti-Sing: Jean Rigby; Peep-Bo: Susan Bullock; Katisha: Felicity Palmer; English National Opera Chorus and Orchestra.

8. The 1990 New D'Oyly Carte recording, conducted by John Pryce-Jones, released by Sony and TER on CD. The Mikado: Michael Ducarel; Nanki-Poo: Bonaventura Bottone; Ko-Ko: Eric Roberts; Pooh-Bah: Malcolm Rivers; Pish-Tush: Gareth Jones; Yum-Yum: Deborah Rees; Pitti-Sing: Thora Ker; Peep-Bo: Yvonne Patrick; Katisha Susan Gorton; New D'Oyly Carte Chorus and Orchestra.

9. The 1992 Welsh National Opera recording, conducted by Charles Mackerras, issued on CD in 1993 by Telarc and in 1999 with all five of the Mackerras G&S Telarc recordings. The Mikado: Donald Adams; Nanki-Poo: Anthony Rolfe Johnson; Ko-Ko: Richard Suart; Pooh-Bah: Richard Van Allan; Pish-Tush: Nicholas Folwell; Yum-Yum: Marie McLaughlin; Pitti-Sing: Anne Howells; Peep-Bo: Janice Watson; Katisha: Felicity Palmer; Welsh National Opera Chorus and Orchestra.

THE MIKADO
Selected Filmography and Videography

1. 1939, film directed by Victor Schertzinger, conducted by Geoffrey Toye, the first time a complete Savoy opera was filmed, available on VHS from Public Media Home Vision, Opera World, on DVD from Image Entertainment, also on CD from Sounds on CD. The Mikado: John Barclay; Nanki-Poo: Kenny Baker; Ko-Ko: Martyn Green; Pooh-Bah: Sydney Granville; Pish-Tush: Gregory Stroud; Yum-Yum: Jean Colin; Pitti-Sing: Elizabeth Paynter; Peep-Bo: Kathleen Naylor; Katisha: Constance Willis; D'Oyly Carte Opera Chorus and Orchestra.

2. 1960, Bell Telephone Hour television production, conducted by Donald Voorhees, condensed to fit in one-hour format, released on LP by Columbia in 1960. The Mikado: Dennis King; Nanki-Poo: Robert Rounseville; Ko-Ko: Groucho Marx; Pooh-Bah: Stanley Holloway; Yum-Yum: Barbara Meister; Pitti-Sing: Sharon Randall; Peep-Bo: Melinda Marx; Katisha: Helen Traubel; Bell Telephone Chorus and Orchestra.

3. 1962, *The Cool Mikado*, set in the 1960s, released on film in 1962, directed by Michael Winner, arranged by Martin Slavin, LP by Parlophone in the, issued on VHS by Fabulous Films, LTD. in 1993. Judge Herbert Mikado: Stubby Kaye; Hank Mikado: Kevin Scott; Ko-Ko: Frankie Howerd; Yum-Yum: Jill Mai Meredith; Pitti-Sing: Yvonne Shima; Peep-Bo: Tsai Chin; Katie Shaw: Jacqueline Jones; Nanki-Poo: Lionel Blair.

4. 1966, film of the D'Oyly Carte Opera performance, conducted by Isidore Godfrey, released on video by British Home Entertainment, reissued in 1994 by Video Artists Guild and in 1996 by Musical Collectibles. The Mikado: Donald Adams; Nanki-Poo: Phillip Potter; Ko-Ko: John Reed; Pooh-Bah: Kenneth Sandford; Pish-Tush: Thomas Lawlor; Yum-Yum: Valerie Masterson; Pitti-Sing: Peggy Ann Jones; Peep-Bo: Pauline Wales; Katisha: Christene Palmer; the D'Oyly Carte Opera Chorus; City of Birmingham Symphony Orchestra.

5. 1982, video of the Brent Walker production, camera direction by Rodney Greenberg, stage direction by Michael Geliot, conducted by Alexander Faris, VHS releases in 1982 by Brent Walker, 1983 by Pioneer Artists, 1986 by Woolworth, 1991 by BraveWorld Video, 1994 by Polygram Video, 1996 by Opera World, 1999 by Roadshow in Australia and New Zealand. The Mikado: William Conrad; Nanki-Poo: John Stewart; Ko-Ko: Clive Revill; Pooh-Bah: Stafford Dean; Pish-Tush: Gordon Sandison; Yum-Yum: Kate Flowers; Pitti-Sing: Cynthia Buchan; Peep-Bo: Fiona Dobie; Katisha: Anne Collins; Ambrosian Opera Chorus; London Symphony Orchestra.

6. 1984, video of the Stratford Festival production, conducted by Berthold Carrière, camera direction by Normal Campbell, stage direction by Brian Madonald, released in 1986 on VHS by Connaiseur and on videodisc by CBC, on VHS in 1998 by Acorn Media, DVD in 1999 by Acorn Media both single and in a three-disc set with *Pirates* and *Iolanthe*. The Mikado: Gidon Saks; Nanki-Poo: Henry Ingram; Ko-Ko: Eric Donkin; Pooh-Bah: Richard McMillan; Pish-Tush: Alan Stewart-Coates; Yum-Yum: Marie Baron; Pitti-Sing: Karen Wood; Peep-Bo: Karen Skidmore; Katisha: Christina James; Stratford Festival Chorus and Orchestra.

7. 1986, video of the English National Opera production set in the 1920s at an English ocean-side hotel, directed by Jonathan Miller, conducted by Peter Robinson, released on VHS by Thames Video and HBO and on video disc by Image Entertainment in 1990, also available on CD. The Mikado: Richard Angas; Nanki-Poo: Bonaventura Bottone; Ko-Ko Eric Idle; Pooh-Bah: Richard Van Allan; Pish-Tush: Mark Richardson; Yum-Yum: Lesley Garrett; Pitti-Sing: Ethna Robinson; Peep-Bo: Susan Bullock; Katisha: Felicity Palmer; English National Opera Chorus and Orchestra.

8. 1988, video of the Australian Opera production, directed by Christopher Renshaw, conducted by Andrew Greene, issued on VHS in 1987 by ABC Video, 1988 by Vision Video Ltd., as well as by Polygram. The Mikado: Robert Eddie; Nanki-Poo: Peter Cousens; Ko-Ko: Graeme Ewer; Pooh-Bah: Gregory Yurisich; Pish-Tush: John Germain; Yum-Yum: Anne-Marie McDonald; Pitti-Sing: Jennifer Bermingham; Peep-Bo: Caroline Clack; Katisha: Heather Begg; Australian Opera Chorus; Elizabethan Sydney Orchestra.

9. 1995, video of the Essgee Entertainment Australian production, stage direction by Craig Schaefer, television direction by Peter Butler, orchestrated and conducted by Kevin Hocking, additional lyrics by Melvyn Morrow, released on VHS in 1995 and 2001 by Essgee Entertainment. The Mikado: David Gould; Nanki-Poo: Derek Metzger; Ko-Ko: Drew Forsyth; Pooh-Bah: Jon English; Pish-Tush: Christophe Broadway; Yum-Yum: Terri Crouch; Katisha: Bev Shean; Three Little Maids (The Fabulous Singlettes): Lisa McArdle, Andrea Gallaher, Georgia Duder.

10. 1999, *Topsy-Turvy*, film directed by Mike Leigh about the creation of *The Mikado*, with many extended scenes of rehearsals and performances, available on VHS and DVD.

11. 2001, Carl Rosa Opera video, conducted by Wyn Davis, released on VHS in 2001 by Carl Rosa. The Mikado: Donald Maxwell; Nanki-Poo: Ivan Sharpe; Ko-Ko: Eric Roberts; Pooh-Bah: Bruce Graham; Pish-Tush: Richard Morrison; Yum-Yum: Mariane Hellgren; Pitti-Sing: Sarah Sweeting; Peep-Bo: Janet Cowley; Katisha: Gillian Knight; the Chorus of Carl Rosa Opera; Carl Rosa Youth Orchestra.

GILBERT'S "BAB" ILLUSTRATIONS

W. S. Gilbert's nickname as a child was "Bab," the family's shortened form for baby. He illustrated each of his librettos with drawings, signed with "Bab." These are some of his illustrations for *The Mikado*.

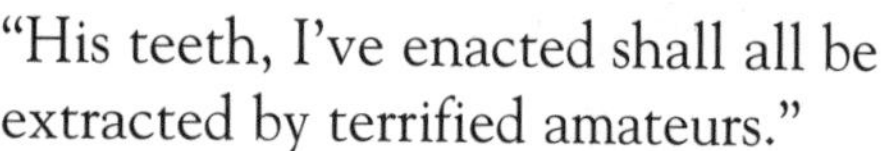

"His teeth, I've enacted shall all be extracted by terrified amateurs."

"And I'm his daughter-in-law elect!" (Katisha)

"The Sun, Whose Rays Are All Ablaze" (Yum-Yum)

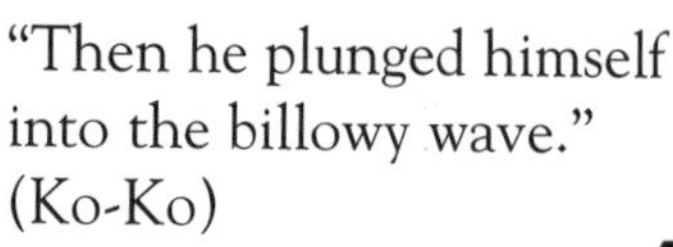

"Then he plunged himself into the billowy wave." (Ko-Ko)

"Each a little bit afraid is, wondering what the world can be!" (Yum-Yum)

"Paint the pretty face, dye the coral lip." (Yum-Yum & Ko-Ko)

The Mikado

"And if you call for a song of the sea, we'll heave the capstan round." (Nanki-Poo)

"Willow, Tit-Willow" (Ko-Ko)

THE MIKADO
or
The Town of Titipu

W. S. Gilbert

Arthur Sullivan

Overture

Allegro ♩=152

*Orchestra material may be rented from the publishers, G. Schirmer, Inc., 609 Fifth Ave., New York, N.Y.

38309 r ×

Printed in the U. S. A.

p
f
sf

Andante comodo

Vi-
a tempo
8
cresc.
- de
rit.
più lento
mf

Allegro con brio 𝅗𝅥 = 112
f
p
1.
2.

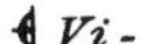 *Vi-*

f

ff

dim.

cresc.

f

dim.

p
p
mf
cresc.
f
dolce
cresc.
p
dim.
p

tr
f
-de
ff
p

tr
mf
p
p
8
8
8
8

8
p
8
cresc. un poco stringendo
8
Più vivo
ff
3

3
ff
sf

ACT I

Scene: *Courtyard of Ko-Ko's Palace in Titipu. Japanese nobles discovered standing and sitting in attitudes suggested by native drawings.*

No. 1. "If you want to know who we are"

Opening Chorus and Recitative

Nanki-Poo and Men

cresc.
ff
Chorus
TENORS & BASSES in Unison
If you want to know who we are,
We are gen-tle-men of Ja - pan:

On_ man-y a vase and jar,_ On_
man-y a screen and fan,_
We fig-ure in live-ly paint: Our at-ti-tude's queer and quaint—You're
wrong if you think it ain't, oh!_

Unison
If you think we are worked by strings
Like a Jap-a-nese mar-io - nette,
You
don't un-der-stand these things:
It is

sim- ply Court et- i - quette.
Per-haps you sup-pose this
throng Can't keep it up all day long? If that's your i - dea, you're
wrong, oh! oh!

TENORS
If that's your i - dea, you're wrong.
BASSES
If that's your i - dea, you're wrong.
ff
If you want to know who we are,
ff
If you want to know who we are,
tr
We are gen-tle-men of Ja - pan:
We are gen-tle-men of Ja - pan:
tr

On vase and jar, On screen and
On vase and jar, On screen and
fan, On man - y, man - y, man - y, man - y, man - y, man - y,
fan, On man - y, man - y, man - y, man - y, man - y, man - y,
fz
fz
man - y, man - y a jar, oh! oh!
sf
man - y, man - y a jar, oh! oh!
fz

sf
oh!
oh!
On
fz
vase and jar, On screen and fan.
sempre ff

Enter Nanki-Poo in great excitement. He carries a native guitar on his back and a bundle of ballads in his hand.
Recit.
Nanki-Poo
Gen-tle-men, I pray you tell me Where a
gen-tle maid-en dwell-eth, Named Yum-Yum, the ward of Ko-Ko:
p
A Noble
In pit-y speak-oh, speak, I pray you! Why, who are you who ask this ques-tion?
Nanki-Poo
Come gath-er round me, and I'll tell you.
p

Segue No. 2

No. 2. "A wand'ring minstrel I"

Solo and Chorus

Nanki-Poo and Men

tune my sup-ple song! I tune my sup - - - ple
Andante espressivo
song! Are you in sen-ti - men-tal mood? I'll sigh with you,
p
Oh, sor - row! On maiden's cold-ness do you brood? I'll
do so, too- Oh, sor-row, sor-row! I'll charm your will-ing

ears With songs of lov-ers' fears,
While sym-pa-thet-ic
cresc.
tears_ My cheeks be-dew—
Oh, sor-row, sor-row!
mf
dim.
Allegro marziale ♩ = 144
But if pa-tri-ot-ic sen-ti-ment is
dim.
p
want-ed, I've pa-tri-ot-ic bal-lads cut and dried;
For wher-

e'er our country's banner may be plant-ed, All oth - er lo-cal banners are de-
fied! Our war-ri-ors, in ser-ried ranks as - sem - bled, Nev- er
quail- or they con-ceal it if they do- And I should-n't be sur-prised if na-tions
trem - bled Be-fore the might - y troops, the troops of Tit - i -
3

pu!
Men
We should-n't be surprised if na - tions trem-bled, trem-bled with a -
larm Be - fore the might-y troops, the troops of Tit - i -
Allegro pesante, non troppo vivo ♪ = 160
Nanki-Poo
pu!
And if you call for a song of the sea, We'll
dim.
heave the cap-stan round, With a yeo heave-ho, for the wind is free, Her

Men
an-chor's a-trip and her helm's a - lee, Hur - rah for the home-ward bound! Yeo -
f
ho, heave - ho, Hur-rah for the home-ward bound!
Nanki-Poo
To lay a-loft in a
p
howl-ing breeze May tick-le a lands-man's taste, But the hap-piest hour a
sail - or sees Is when he's down At an in - land town, With his

TENORS
Nan-cy on his knees, yeo-ho! And his arm a-round her waist! Then
BASSES
Then
man the cap-stan— off we go, As the fid-dler swings us round, With a
man the cap-stan— off we go, As the fid-dler swings us round, With a
yeo heave-ho, And a rum be-low, Hur-rah for the home-ward bound!— With a
yeo heave-ho, And a rum be-low, Hur-rah for the home-ward bound!— With a

yeo heave-ho, And a rum be-low, Yeo-
yeo heave-ho, And a rum be-low, Yeo-
f
ho, heave-ho, Yeo-ho, heave-ho, heave-ho, heave-ho, yeo-
ho, heave-ho, Yeo-ho, heave-ho, heave-ho, heave-ho, yeo-
cresc.
ho!
ho!
ff
dim.

(Enter Pish-Tush.)

Pish: And what may be your business with Yum-Yum?

Nanki: I'll tell you. A year ago I was a member of the Titipu town band. It was my duty to take the cap round for contributions. While discharging this delicate office, I saw Yum-Yum. We loved each other at once, but she was betrothed to her guardian, Ko-Ko, a cheap tailor, and I saw that my suit was hopeless. Overwhelmed with despair, I quitted the town. Judge of my delight when I heard, a month ago, that Ko-Ko had been condemned to death for flirting! I hurried back at once, in the hope of finding Yum-Yum at liberty to listen to my protestations.

Pish: It is true that Ko-Ko was condemned to death for flirting, but he was reprieved at the last moment, and raised to the exalted rank of Lord High Executioner under the following remarkable circumstances:

No. 3. "Our great Mikado, virtuous man"

Solo and Chorus

Pish-Tush and Men

Allegretto con brio ♩= 126
f
dim.
Pish-Tush
Our great Mi-ka-do, vir-tuous man, When he to rule our
p
land be-gan, Re-solved to try A plan where-by Young men might best be
stead-ied. So he de-creed, in words suc-cinct, That all who flirt-ed,

leered, or winked (Un - less con - nu - bi - al - ly linked), Should forth-with be be -
head-ed, be-head-ed, be - head - - - ed, Should forth-with
be be - head-ed.
ff
2 3 1
And I ex-pect you'll all a-gree That he was right to so de-cree. And
p

I am right, And you are right, And all is right as right can be!
Men
f
And
you are right, And we are right, And all is right, is right as right can
f
Pish-Tush
And all is right as right can be, right as right can
be! And all is right as right can be, right as right can
be!
be!
ff

Pish-Tush
This
dim.
stern de-cree, you'll un-der-stand, Caused great dis-may through-out the land: For
p
young and old And shy and bold Were e-qual-ly af-fect-ed. The
youth who winked a rov-ing eye, Or breathed a non-con-nu-bial sigh, Was

there-up-on con-demned to die— He— u-sual-ly ob-ject-ed, ob-
ject-ed, ob-ject - - - ed, He u-sual-ly ob-ject-ed.
ff
And you'll al-low, as
p
I ex-pect, That he was right to so ob-ject. And I am right, And

you are right, And ev - 'ry-thing is quite cor-rect!
Men
And you are right, And
And ev-'ry -
we are right, And ev - 'ry-thing is quite, is quite cor - rect, And ev-'ry -
thing is quite cor-rect, All is quite cor - rect!
thing is quite cor-rect, All is quite cor - rect!
Pish-Tush
And

so we straight let out on bail A con-vict from the coun-ty jail, Whose
p
head was next, On some pre-text, Con-demn-ed to be mown off, And
made him Heads-man, for we said, "Who's next to be de-cap-it-ed Can-
not cut off an-oth-er's head Un-til he's cut his own off, his own off, his

own off, Un-til he's cut his own off."
ff
And
we are right, I think you'll say, To ar-gue in this kind of way. And
p
I am right, And you are right, And all is right—too - loo-ral-lay!
Men
f
And

you are right, And we are right, And all is right— too-
f
And I am right, And you are
loo - ral, loo - ral - lay! And you are right, And we are
rall.
a tempo
right, And all is right!
rall.
a tempo
right, And all is right!
rall.
ff a tempo

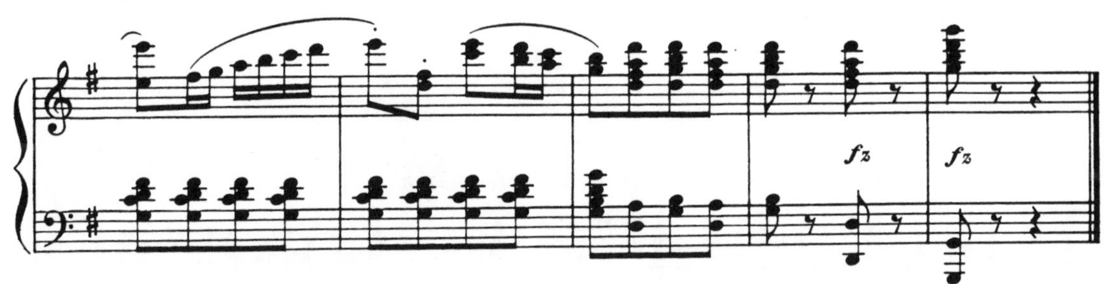

(Exeunt Chorus. Enter Pooh-Bah.)

Nanki: Ko-Ko, the cheap tailor, Lord High Executioner of Titipu! Why, that's the highest rank a citizen can attain!

Pooh: It is. Our logical Mikado, seeing no moral difference between the dignified judge who condemns a criminal to die, and the industrious mechanic who carries out the sentence, has rolled the two offices into one, and every judge is now his own executioner.

Nanki: But how good of you (for I see that you are a nobleman of the highest rank) to condescend to tell all this to me, a mere strolling minstrel!

Pooh: Don't mention it. I am, in point of fact, a particularly haughty and exclusive person, of pre-Adamite ancestral descent. You will understand this when I tell you that I can trace my ancestry back to a protoplasmal primordial atomic globule. Consequently, my family pride is something inconceivable. I can't help it. I was born sneering. But I struggle hard to overcome this defect. I mortify my pride continually. When all the great Officers of State resigned in a body because they were too proud to serve under an ex-tailor, did I not unhesitatingly accept all their posts at once?

Pish: And the salaries attached to them? You did.

Pooh: It is consequently my degrading duty to serve this upstart as First Lord of the Treasury, Lord Chief Justice, Commander-in-Chief, Lord High Admiral, Master of the Buckhounds, Groom of the Back Stairs, Archbishop of Titipu, and Lord Mayor, both acting and elect, all rolled into one. And at a salary! A Pooh-Bah paid for his services! I a salaried minion! But I do it! It revolts me, but I do it.

Nanki: And it does you credit.

Pooh: But I don't stop at that. I go and dine with middle-class people on reasonable terms. I dance at cheap suburban parties for a moderate fee. I accept refreshment at any hands, however lowly. I also retail State secrets at a very low figure. For instance, any further information about Yum-Yum would come under the head of a State secret. *(Nanki-Poo takes the hint, and gives him money.)* *(Aside),* Another insult, and I think a light one!

No. 4. "Young man, despair"

Song

Pooh-Bah, Nanki-Poo, and Pish-Tush

lu - tion-er!
This ver - y day From school Yum-
Yum
Will wend her way, And home-ward
come, With beat of drum, And a rum - - tum-tum, To wed the
Lord High Ex - e - cu - tion-er!

ff
p
And the brass will crash, And the trum-pets bray, And they'll cut a dash On their wed-ding
day. She'll tod-dle a-way, as all a-ver, With the Lord High Ex-e-
cu-tion-er!
Nanki-Poo and Pish-Tush
And the brass will crash, And the trum-pets bray, And they'll cut a dash On their wed-ding
She'll tod-dle a-way, as all a-ver, With the Lord High Ex-e-
day. She'll tod-dle a-way, as all a-ver, With the Lord High Ex-e-

cu-tion-er!
cu-tion-er!
Pooh-Bah
It's a hope-less case, As you may see, And in your place A -
way I'd flee; But don't blame me— I'm sor-ry to be Of your plea - sure a dim - i -
nu - tion-er. They'll vow their pact Ex-treme-ly

soon,
In point of fact This af - ter-
noon Her hon - - ey-moon With that buf-foon At seven com-
men - ces, so you shun her!
And the brass will crash, And the trum-pets bray, And they'll cut a dash On their wed-ding

day. She'll tod-dle a-way, as all a-ver, With the Lord High Ex-e-

cu-tion-er!

Nanki-Poo and Pish-Tush

And the brass will crash, And the trum-pets bray, And they'll cut a dash On their wed-ding

She'll tod-dle a-way, as all a-ver, With the Lord High Ex-e-

day. She'll tod-dle a-way, as all a-ver, With the Lord High Ex-e-

cu-tion-er!

cu-tion-er!

(Exit Pish-Tush.)

No. 4a. "And have I journeyed for a month"

Recitative

Nanki-Poo and Pooh-Bah

Nanki-Poo
Recitative
And have I jour-neyed for a month, or near-ly, To learn that Yum-Yum,
p
whom I love so dear-ly, This day to Ko-Ko is to be u - nit - ed!
f
Pooh-Bah Recitative
The fact ap-pears to be as you've re-cit - ed:
dim.
p
Moderato
Recitative
But here he comes, e -
p
3
3
quipped as suits his sta-tion; He'll give you an-y fur-ther in-for - ma - tion.

Attacca No. 5

(Exeunt Pooh-Bah and Nanki-Poo. Enter Chorus of Nobles.)

No. 5. "Behold the Lord High Executioner"

Chorus and Solo

Ko-Ko and Men

per-son-age of no-ble rank and ti - tle— A dig-ni-fied and po-tent
per-son-age of no-ble rank and ti - tle— A dig-ni-fied and po-tent
of-fi-cer, Whose func-tions are par-tic - u-lar-ly vi - tal! De-
of-fi-cer, Whose func-tions are par-tic - u-lar-ly vi - tal! De-
fer, de-fer, To the Lord High Ex-e - cu-tion-er! De-
fer, de-fer, To the Lord High Ex-e - cu-tion-er! De-

fer, ——— de - fer, ——— To the no - ble Lord, to the

fer, ——— de - fer, ——— To the no - ble Lord, to the

no - ble Lord, to the Lord High — Ex - e - cu - tion - er!

no - ble Lord, to the Lord High — Ex - e - cu - tion - er!

(Enter Ko-Ko, attended.)

Ko-Ko

Ta-ken from the coun-ty jail By a set of cu - rious

p

chan-ces; Lib-er-at-ed then on bail,

On my own re-cog-ni - zan-ces; Waft-ed by a fav-'ring gale,
As one some-times is in tran-ces, To a height that few can scale,
Save by long and wea - ry dan-ces; Sure-ly, nev-er had a male
Un-der such like cir-cum-stan-ces So ad - ven-tur-ous a tale, Which may

rank with most ro - man-ces.
Ta-ken from the coun-ty jail
p
Ta-ken from the coun-ty
p
Ta-ken from the coun-ty
p cresc.
By a set of cu-rious chan - ces;
Sure-ly, nev-er had a
jail,
Lib-er-at - ed then on bail;
Sure-ly, nev-er
jail,
Lib-er-at - ed then on bail;
Sure-ly, nev-er
male So ad-ven - tur - ous a tale.
had a male So ad-ven - tur - ous a tale. De-
f
had a male So ad-ven - tur - ous a tale. De-
f

fer, — de-fer, — To the Lord High Ex-e - cu-tion-er! De-
fer, — 'de-fer, — To the Lord High Ex-e - cu-tion-er! De-
fer, — de-fer, — To the no-ble Lord, to the no-ble Lord High
fer, — de-fer, — To the no-ble Lord, to the no-ble Lord High
Ex-e - cu - tion - er! Bow down, bow down, — To the
Ex-e - cu - tion - er! Bow down, bow down, — To the
ff

Ko: Gentlemen, I'm much touched by this reception. I can only trust that by strict attention to duty I shall ensure a continuance of those favours which it will ever be my study to deserve. If I should ever be called upon to act professionally, I am happy to think that there will be no difficulty in finding plenty of people whose loss will be a distinct gain to society at large.

No. 5a. "As some day it may happen"

Solo and Chorus

Ko-Ko and Men

nev - er would be missed— who nev - er would be missed! There's the
nev - er would be missed— they nev - er would be missed! Then the
pes - ti - len - tial nui - san - ces who write for au - to-graphs— All
id - i - ot who prais-es, with en - thu - si - as - tic tone, All
peo - ple who have flab - by hands and ir - ri - tat - ing laughs— All
cen - tu - ries but this, and ev - 'ry coun-try but his own; And the
chil-dren who are up in dates, and floor you with 'em flat— All
la - dy from the prov - in - ces, who dress - es like a guy, And "who

per-sons who in shak-ing hands, shake hands with you like *that*— And
does-n't think she danc-es, but would rath-er like to try"; And that
all third per-sons who on spoil-ing *tête-à-têtes* in-sist— They'd
sin-gu-lar a-nom-a-ly, the la-dy nov-el-ist— I
Chorus of Men
none of 'em be missed— they'd none of 'em be missed! He's
don't think she'd be missed— I'm *sure* she'd not be missed! He's
He's
He's
f
got 'em on the list— he's got 'em on the list; And they'll
got her on the list— he's got her on the list; And I
got 'em on the list— he's got 'em on the list; And they'll
got her on the list— he's got her on the list; And I

Ko-Ko
none of 'em be missed– they'll none of 'em be missed! 2. There's the
don't think she'll be missed– I'm *sure* she'll not be missed! 3. And that
none of 'em be missed– they'll none of 'em be missed!
don't think she'll be missed– I'm *sure* she'll not be missed!
Ni - si Pri - us nui-sance, who just now is rath - er rife, The Ju -
di - cial hu - mor - ist– I've got *him* on the list! All
fun - ny fel - lows, com - ic men, and clowns of pri - vate life– They'd

none of 'em be missed— they'd none of 'em be missed! And a-
pol-o-get-ic states-men of a com-pro-mis-ing kind, Such as—
What d'ye call him—Thing-'em-bob, and like-wise—Nev-er mind, And
colla voce
'St— 'st— 'st— and What's-his-name, and al-so You-know-who— The
task of fill-ing up the blanks I'd rath-er leave to *you.* But it

real - ly does - n't mat - ter whom you put up - on the list, For they'd none of 'em be missed— they'd none of 'em be missed!

Chorus of Men

You may put 'em on the list— you may put 'em on the list; And they'll none of 'em be missed— they'll none of 'em be missed!

You may put 'em on the list— you may put 'em on the list; And they'll none of 'em be missed— they'll none of 'em be missed!

f

f

(Exeunt Chorus. Enter Pooh-Bah.)

Ko: Pooh-Bah, it seems that the festivities in connection with my approaching marriage must last a week. I should like to do it handsomely, and I want to consult you as to the amount I ought to spend upon them.

Pooh: Certainly. In which of my capacities? As First Lord of the Treasury, Lord Chamberlain, Attorney-General, Chancellor of the Exchequer, Privy Purse, or Private Secretary?

Ko: Suppose we say as Private Secretary.

Pooh: Speaking as your Private Secretary, I should say that as the city will have to pay for it, don't stint yourself, do it well.

Ko: Exactly— as the city will have to pay for it. That is your advice.

Pooh: As Private Secretary. Of course you will understand that, as Chancellor of the Exchequer, I am bound to see that due economy is observed.

Ko: Oh! But you said just now "Don't stint yourself, do it well".

Pooh: As Private Secretary.

Ko: And now you say that due economy must be observed.

Pooh: As Chancellor of the Exchequer.

Ko: I see. Come over here, where the Chancellor can't hear us. *(They cross the stage.)* Now, as my Solicitor, how do you advise me to deal with this difficulty?

Pooh: Oh, as your Solicitor, I should have no hesitation in saying "Chance it—"

Ko: Thank you. *(Shaking his hand)* I will.

Pooh: If it were not that, as Lord Chief Justice, I am bound to see that the law isn't violated.

Ko: I see. Come over here, where the Chief Justice can't hear us. *(They cross the stage.)* Now, then, as First Lord of the Treasury?

Pooh: Of course, as First Lord of the Treasury, I could propose a special vote that would cover all expenses, if it were not that, as Leader of the Opposition, it would be my duty to resist it, tooth and nail. Or, as Paymaster-General, I could so cook the accounts that, as Lord High Auditor, I should never discover the fraud. But then, as Archbishop of Titipu, it would be my duty to denounce my dishonesty and give myself into my own custody as First Commissioner of Police.

Ko: That's extremely awkward.

Pooh: I don't say that all these distinguished people couldn't be squared; but it is right to tell you that they wouldn't be sufficiently degraded in their own estimation unless they are insulted with a very considerable bribe.

Ko: The matter shall have my careful consideration. But my bride and her sisters approach, and any little compliment on your part, such as an abject grovel in a characteristic Japanese attitude, would be esteemed a favour.

(Exeunt together. Enter procession of Yum-Yum's schoolfellows, heralding Yum-Yum, Peep-Bo, and Pitti-Sing.)

No. 6. "Comes a train of little ladies"

Chorus

Girls

Girls
Comes a — train of lit - tle la - dies
From scho - las - tic — tram - mels free,
Each a lit - tle bit a - fraid is, Won - d'ring
what the world can be!

Is it but a world of trou - ble—
Sad - ness set to song?
f
Is its beau - ty but a bub - ble
f
Is its beau - ty but a bub - ble
p
Bound to break ere long?
p
Bound to break ere long?

f
Are its pal - a - ces and plea - sures
f
Are its
Fan - ta - sies that fade?
plea - sures Fan - ta - sies that fade?
And the glo - ry of its trea - sures
And the glo - ry of its
Shad - ow of a shade?
trea - sures Shad - ow of a shade?
f

dim.
And the glo - ry of its trea - sures
And the glo - ry of its trea - sures
dim.
Shad - ow of a shade?
Shad - ow of a shade?
p
Ped.
p
Shad - ow of a shade?
dim.
f
School-girls we, eight - een and un - der,
f
School-girls we, eight - een and un - der,
p

From scho - las - tic tram - mels free, And we
won - der— how we won - der!— We won - der— how we
won - der!— What on earth the world can
dim.
fz
be! What on earth the world can be!
rit.
p
a tempo
mf
Attacca No. 7

No. 7. "Three little maids from school are we"

Trio and Chorus

Yum-Yum, Peep-Bo, Pitti-Sing, and Girls

Three lit-tle maids from school! Ev-'ry-thing is a source of_ fun. (Chuckle)
Three lit-tle maids from school!
Three lit-tle maids from school!
Peep-Bo
No-bod-y's safe, for we care for_ none! (Chuckle)
Pitti-Sing
Life is a joke that's just be-gun! (Chuckle)
Yum-Yum
Three lit-tle maids from school!
Peep-Bo
Three lit-tle maids from school!
Pitti-Sing
Three lit-tle maids from school!
p

(Dancing)
Three lit-tle maids who, all un-wa-ry,
Three lit-tle maids who, all un-wa-ry,
Three lit-tle maids who, all un-wa-ry,
fz
p
Come from a la-dies' sem-i-na-ry, Freed from its ge-nius
Come from a la-dies' sem-i-na-ry, Freed from its ge-nius
Come from a la-dies' sem-i-na-ry, Freed from its ge-nius
(Suddenly demure)
tu-te-la-ry— Three lit-tle maids from school!
tu-te-la-ry— Three lit-tle maids from school!
tu-te-la-ry— Three lit-tle maids from school!

fz
Three lit-tle maids — from school!
fz
Three lit-tle maids — from school!
fz
Three lit-tle maids — from school!
Yum-Yum
One lit-tle maid is a bride, Yum-Yum —
p
Peep-Bo
Two lit-tle maids in at-ten-dance come —
Pitti-Sing
Three lit-tle maids is the to-tal sum.

Yum-Yum
Three lit-tle maids from school!
From
Peep-Bo
Three lit-tle maids from school!
Pitti-Sing
Three lit-tle maids from school!
p
three lit-tle maids take one a-way—
Two lit-tle maids re-main, and they—
Three lit-tle maids from school!
Three lit-tle maids from school!
Won't have to wait ver-y long, they say—
Three lit-tle maids from school!

(Dancing)
Three lit-tle maids who, all un-wa-ry,
Three lit-tle maids who, all un-wa-ry,
Three lit-tle maids who, all un-wa-ry,
Chorus of Girls
Three lit-tle maids from school!
Three lit-tle maids who, all un-wa-ry,
cresc.
p
Come from a la-dies' sem-i-na-ry, Freed from its ge-nius tu-te-la-ry—
Come from a la-dies' sem-i-na-ry, Freed from its ge-nius tu-te-la-ry—
Come from a la-dies' sem-i-na-ry, Freed from its ge-nius tu-te-la-ry—
Come from a la-dies' sem-i-na-ry, Freed from its ge-nius tu-te-la-ry—

(Enter Ko-Ko and Pooh-Bah.)

Ko: At last, my bride that is to be! *(About to embrace her)*

Yum: You're not going to kiss me before all these people!

Ko: Well, that was the idea.

Yum: *(aside to Peep-Bo)* It seems odd, doesn't it?

Peep: It's rather peculiar.

Pitti: Oh, I expect it's all right. Must have a beginning, you know.

Yum: Well, of course I know nothing about these things; but I've no objection if it's usual.

Ko: Oh, it's quite usual, I think. Eh, Lord Chamberlain? *(Appealing to Pooh-Bah)*

Pooh: I have known it done. *(Ko-Ko embraces her.)*

Yum: Thank goodness that's over! *(Sees Nanki-Poo and rushes to him)* Why, that's never you! *(The Three Girls rush to him and shake his hands, all speaking at once.)*

Yum: Oh, I'm so glad! I haven't seen you for ever so long, and I'm right at the top of the school, and I've got three prizes, and I've come home for good, and I'm not going back any more!

Peep: And have you got an engagement? Yum-Yum's got one, but she doesn't like it, and she'd ever so much rather it was you. I've come home for good, and I'm not going back any more!

Pitti: Now tell us all the news, because you go about everywhere, and we've been at school, but, thank goodness, that's all over now, and we've come home for good, and we're not going back any more!

(These three speeches are spoken together in one breath.)

Ko: I beg your pardon. Will you present me?

Yum: Oh, this is the musician who used—

Peep: Oh, this is the gentleman who used—

Pitti: Oh, it is only Nanki-Poo who used—

Ko: One at a time, if you please.

Yum: Oh, if you please, he's the gentleman who used to play so beautifully on the— on the—

Pitti: On the Marine Parade.

Yum: Yes, I think that was the name of the instrument.

Nanki: Sir, I have the misfortune to love your ward, Yum-Yum— oh, I know I deserve your anger!

Ko: Anger! not a bit, my boy. Why, I love her myself. Charming little girl, isn't she? Pretty eyes, nice hair. Taking little thing, altogether. Very glad to hear my opinion backed by a competent authority. Thank you very much. Good-bye. *(To Pish-Tush)* Take him away. *(Pish-Tush removes him.)*

Pitti: *(who has been examining Pooh-Bah)* I beg your pardon, but what is this? Customer come to try on?

Ko: That is a Tremendous Swell.

Pitti: Oh, it's alive. *(She starts back in alarm.)*

Pooh: Go away, little girls. Can't talk to little girls like you. Go away, there's dears.

Ko: Allow me to present you, Pooh-Bah. These are my three wards. The one in the middle is my bride-elect.

Pooh: What do you want me to do to them? Mind, I *will not* kiss them.

Ko: No, no, you shan't kiss them: a little bow— a mere nothing— you needn't mean it, you know.

Pooh: It goes against the grain. They are not young ladies, they are young persons.

Ko: Come, come, make an effort, there's a good nobleman.

Pooh: *(aside to Ko-Ko)* Well, I shan't mean it. *(With a great effort)* How de do, little girls, how de do? *(Aside)* Oh, my protoplasmal ancestor!

Ko: That's very good. *(Girls indulge in suppressed laughter.)*

Pooh: I see nothing to laugh at. It is very painful to me to have to say "How de do, little girls, how de do?" to young persons. I'm not in the habit of saying "How de do, little girls, how de do?" to anybody under the rank of a Stockbroker.

Ko: *(aside to girls)* Don't laugh at him, he can't help it— he's under treatment for it. *(Aside to Pooh-Bah)* Never mind them, they don't understand the delicacy of your position.

Pooh: We know how delicate it is, don't we?

Ko: I should think we did! How a nobleman of your importance can do it at all is a thing I never can, never shall understand.

(Ko-Ko retires up and goes off.)

No. 8. "So please you, Sir, we much regret"

Quartet and Chorus

Yum-Yum, Peep-Bo, Pitti-Sing, Pooh-Bah, and Girls

wards a man of rank so high—We shall know bet-ter by and by. But
wards a man of rank so high—We shall know bet-ter by and by.
wards a man of rank so high—We shall know bet-ter by and by.
youth, of course, must have its fling, So par-don us, So par-don us,
Pitti-Sing
And
don't, in girl-hood's hap-py spring, Be hard on us, Be hard on us, If

(Dancing)
Yum-Yum
But
Peep-Bo
But
we're in-clined to dance and sing, Tra la la la la la, But
Chorus of Girls
Tra la la la la la, Tra la la la la
youth, of course, must have its fling, So par-don us, And
youth, of course, must have its fling, So par-don us, And
youth, of course, must have its fling, So par-don us, And
la, Tra la la la la la, Tra la la la la la, Tra la la la la la, Tra la la la la

don't, in girl - hood's hap - py spring, Be hard on us.
don't, in girl - hood's hap - py spring, Be hard on us.
don't, in girl - hood's hap - py spring, Be hard on us.
la, Tra la la la la la, Tra la la la la la, Tra la la la la la! But
f
f
Tra la la la la la la
Tra la la la la la la
Tra la la la la la la
youth, of course, must have its fling, So par - don us, Tra la la la la la la

la la, Tra la la la la la la la, Tra la la la la la la la la, Tra la la la la
la la, Tra la la la la la la la, Tra la la la la la la la la, Tra la la la la
la la, Tra la la la la la la la, Tra la la la la la la la la, Tra la la la la
la la, Tra la la la la la la la, Tra la la la la la la la la, Tra la la la la
fz
la la la la, Tra la la la la la la la la la la la la la la la!
la la la la, Tra la la la la la la la la la la la la la la la!
la la la la, Tra la la la la la la la la la la la la la la la!
la la la la, Tra la la la la la la la la la la la la la la la!
f

Pooh-Bah
I think you ought to re-col - lect You can-not
show too much re - spect To-wards the high-ly ti - tled few; But no - bod - y
does, and why should you! That youth at us should have its fling, Is
p

hard on us, Is hard on us; To our pre-rog-a-tive we cling— So
pardon us, So pardon us, If we de-cline to dance and
(Dancing)
Yum-Yum
But youth, of
Peep-Bo
But youth, of
Pitti-Sing
But youth, of
sing. Tra la la la la la, Tra la la la la la, Tra la la la la

course, must have its fling, So par - don us, And
course, must have its fling, So par - don us, And
course, must have its fling, So par - don us, And
la, Tra la la la la la, Tra la la la la la, Tra la la la la

don't, in girl - hood's hap - py spring, Be
don't, in girl - hood's hap - py spring, Be
don't, in girl - hood's hap - py spring, Be
la, Tra la la la la la, Tra la la la la la, Tra la la la la

hard on us.
Tra
hard on us.
Tra
hard on us.
Tra
la la la!
Tra
Chorus
f
But youth, of course, must have its fling, So par - don us, Tra
f
la la la la la la la la, Tra la la la la la la la, Tra
la la la la la la la la, Tra la la la la la la la, Tra
la la la la la la la la, Tra la la la la la la la, Tra
la la la la la la la la, Tra la la la la la la la, Tra
la la la la la la la la, Tra la la la la la la la, Tra
fz

la la la la la la la la, Tra la la la la la la la la,
la la la la la la la la, Tra la la la la la la la la,
la la la la la la la la, Tra la la la la la la la la,
la la la la la la la la, Tra la la la la la la la la,
la la la la la la la la, Tra la la la la la la la la,
fz
Tra la la la la la la la la la la la la la la!
Tra la la la la la la la la la la la la la la!
Tra la la la la la la la la la la la la la la!
Tra la la la la la la la la la la la la la la!
Tra la la la la la la la la la la la la la la!
f

(Exeunt all but Yum-Yum. Enter Nanki-Poo.)

Nanki: Yum-Yum, at last we are alone! I have sought you night and day for three weeks, in the belief that your guardian was beheaded, and I find that you are about to be married to him this afternoon!

Yum: Alas, yes!

Nanki: But you do not love him?

Yum: Alas, no!

Nanki: Modified rapture! But why do you not refuse him?

Yum: What good would that do? He's my guardian, and he wouldn't let me marry you.

Nanki: But I would wait until you were of age!

Yum: You forget that in Japan girls do not arrive at years of discretion until they are fifty.

Nanki: True; from seventeen to forty-nine are considered years of indiscretion.

Yum: Besides— a wandering minstrel, who plays a wind instrument outside tea-houses, is hardly a fitting husband for the ward of a Lord High Executioner.

Nanki: But— *(Aside)* Shall I tell her? Yes! She will not betray me! *(Aloud)* What if it should prove that, after all, I am no musician!

Yum: There! I was certain of it, directly I heard you play!

Nanki: What if it should prove that I am no other than the son of his Majesty the Mikado?

Yum: The son of the Mikado! But why is your Highness disguised? And what has your Highness done? And will your Highness promise never to do it again?

Nanki: Some years ago I had the misfortune to captivate Katisha, an elderly lady of my father's Court. She misconstrued my customary affability into expressions of affection, and claimed me in marriage, under my father's law. My father, the Lucius Junius Brutus of his race, ordered me to marry her within a week, or perish ignominiously on the scaffold. That night I fled his Court, and, assuming the disguise of a Second Trombone, I joined the band in which you found me when I had the happiness of seeing you! *(Approaching her)*

Yum: *(retreating)* If you please, I think your Highness had better not come too near. The laws against flirting are excessively severe.

Nanki: But we are quite alone, and nobody can see us.

Yum: Still, that doesn't make it right. To flirt is capital.

Nanki: It *is* capital!

Yum: And we must obey the law.

Nanki: Deuce take the law!

Yum: I wish it would, but it won't!

Nanki: If it were not for that, how happy we might be!

Yum: Happy indeed!

Nanki: If it were not for the law, we should now be sitting side by side, like that. *(Sits by her)*

Yum: Instead of being obliged to sit half a mile off, like that. *(Crosses and sits at other side of stage)*

Nanki: We should be gazing into each other's eyes, like that. *(Approaching and gazing at her sentimentally)*

Yum: Breathing sighs of unutterable love— like that. *(Sighing and gazing lovingly at him)*

Nanki: With our arms round each other's waists, like that. *(Embracing her)*

Yum: Yes, if it wasn't for the law.

Nanki: If it wasn't for the law.

Yum: As it is, of course we couldn't do anything of the kind.

Nanki: Not for worlds!

Yum: Being engaged to Ko-Ko, you know!

Nanki: Being engaged to Ko-Ko!

No. 9. "Were you not to Ko-Ko plighted"

Duet

Yum-Yum and Nanki-Poo

Yum-Yum
(Kiss)
Allegro ♩ = 132
He would kiss me fond-ly thus— But as I'm en-gaged to Ko-Ko,
thus—(Kissing her) I would kiss you fond-ly thus—
p
To em-brace you thus, con fuo-co, Would dis-tinct-ly be no gio-co,
And for that I should get to-co, To-co, to-co,
Nanki
To-co, to-co,
to-co, to-co, to-co!
to-co, to-co, to-co! So, in spite of all temp-
f

Tempo I°
Nanki
ta - tion, Such a theme I'll not dis-cuss, And on no con-sid-er-
a - tion Will I kiss you fond - ly thus— Will I kiss you fond - ly
(Kissing her)
colla voce
dim.
Allegro
thus. Let me make it clear to you, This is what I'll nev-er do, This, oh,
this— oh, this— oh, this— This ___ is what I'll nev - er,—
(Kissing her)
fz

Yum-Yum

This, oh, this— oh, this— oh, this— this,—

nev - er do! This, oh, this— oh, this— oh, this— this—

fz

He'll nev - er do! He'll

— is what I'll nev - er do! I'll nev - er do!

cresc.

nev-er do! This is what he'll nev - er, nev - er do!

Oh, this, this is what I'll nev - er, nev - er do!

vivo

f

ff

(Exeunt in opposite directions. Enter Ko-Ko.)

Ko: *(looking after Yum-Yum)* There she goes! To think how entirely my future happiness is wrapped up in that little parcel! Really, it hardly seems worth while! Oh, matrimony!— *(Enter Pooh-Bah and Pish-Tush.)* Now then, what is it? Can't you see I'm soliloquizing? You have interrupted an apostrophe, sir!

Pish: I am the bearer of a letter from his Majesty, the Mikado.

Ko: *(taking it from him reverentially)* A letter from the Mikado! What in the world can he have to say to me? *(Reads letter)* Ah, here it is at last! I thought it would come sooner or later! The Mikado is struck by the fact that no executions have taken place in Titipu for a year, and decrees that unless somebody is beheaded within one month, the post of Lord High Executioner shall be abolished, and the city reduced to the rank of a village!

Pish: But that will involve us all in irretrievable ruin!

Ko: Yes. There is no help for it, I shall have to execute somebody at once. The only question is, who shall it be?

Pooh: Well, it seems unkind to say so, but as you're already under sentence of death for flirting, everything seems to point to *you.*

Ko: To me? What are you talking about? I can't execute myself.

Pooh: Why not?

Ko: Why not? Because, in the first place, self-decapitation is an extremely difficult, not to say dangerous, thing to attempt; and, in the second, it's suicide, and suicide is a capital offence.

Pooh: That is so, no doubt.

Pish: We might reserve that point.

Pooh: True, it could be argued six months hence, before the full Court.

Ko: Besides, I don't see how a man *can* cut off his own head.

Pooh: A man might try.

Pish: Even if you only succeeded in cutting it half off, that would be something.

Pooh: It would be taken as an earnest of your desire to comply with the Imperial will.

Ko: No. Pardon me, but there I am adamant. As official Headsman, my reputation is at stake, and I can't consent to embark on a professional operation unless I see my way to a successful result.

Pooh: This professional conscientiousness is highly creditable to *you*, but it places us in a very awkward position.

Ko: My good sir, the awkwardness of your position is grace itself compared with that of a man engaged in the act of cutting off his own head.

Pish: I am afraid that, unless you can obtain a substitute—

Ko: A substitute? Oh, certainly— nothing easier. *(To Pooh-Bah)* Pooh-Bah, I appoint you Lord High Substitute.

Pooh: I should be delighted. Such an appointment would realize my fondest dreams. But no, at any sacrifice, I must set bounds to my insatiable ambition!

No. 10. "I am so proud"

Trio

Pooh-Bah, Ko-Ko, and Pish-Tush

Ko-Ko
My brain it teems — With end-less schemes, Both good and new, For Tit - i -
p
pu, For Tit-i - pu; But if I flit, The ben-e-fit That I'd dif-fuse The town would lose! Now
ev'ry man To aid his clan Should plot and plan As best he can.
p
Pish-Tush
I heard one day A gen-tle-man say That crim-i-nals who Are

cut in two Can hard - ly feel The fa - tal steel, And so are slain, are
slain With-out much pain. If this is true, It's jol - ly for you; Your cour - age
screw To bid us a-dieu.
Pooh-Bah
I
sf
Pish-Tush
I heard one day A
Ko-Ko
My brain it teems With end-less
am so proud, If I al - lowed My

gen-tle-man say That crim-i-nals who Are cut in two Can hard-ly feel The
schemes, Both good and new, For Tit-i - pu, For Tit-i - pu; But if I
fam-i-ly pride To be my guide, I'd
fa-tal steel, And so are slain, are slain With-out _ much pain. If this is
flit, The ben-e-fit That I'd dif-fuse The town would lose! Now
vol-un-teer To quit this sphere, In-
true, It's jol-ly for you; Your cour-age screw To bid us a-dieu.
ev-'ry man To aid his clan Should plot and plan As best he can.
stead of you, In a min-ute or two.

Ko-Ko
And so, Al-though I'm read-y to go, Yet
re-col-lect 'Twere dis-re-spect Did I neg-lect To thus ef-fect This
aim di-rect, So I ob-ject—
Pooh-Bah
And so, Al-though I
wish to go, And great-ly pine To bright-ly shine, And

Pish-Tush
And
rit.
take the line Of a he-ro fine, With grief con-dign I must de-cline—
rit.
a tempo
go And show Both friend and foe How much you dare. I'm quite a-ware It's
a tempo
your af-fair, Yet I de-clare I'd take your share, But I don't much
care— I'd take your share, But I don't much care, I'd
Ko-Ko
So I ob - ject, So I ob -
Pooh-Bah
I must de - cline, I must de -

take your share, But I don't much care, I'd take your share, But I don't much care, much
ject, So I ob - ject, So I ob -
cline, I must de - cline, I must de -
care, I don't much care, I don't much care— To
ject, So I ob - ject, So I ob - ject— To
cline, I must de - cline, I must de - cline— To
p
Un poco più vivo
sit in sol - emn si - lence in a dull, dark dock, In a
marcato

pes- ti - len-tial pris - on, with a life - long lock, A - wait - ing the sen - sa - tion of a
pes- ti - len-tial pris - on, with a life - long lock, A - wait - ing the sen - sa - tion of a
pes- ti - len-tial pris - on, with a life - long lock, A - wait - ing the sen - sa - tion of a
short, sharp shock, From a cheap and chip - py chop-per on a big black block! To
short, sharp shock, From a cheap and chip - py chop-per on a big black block! To
short, sharp shock, From a cheap and chip - py chop-per on a big black block! To
sit in sol-emn si-lence in a dull, dark dock, In a pes- ti - len-tial pris - on, with a
sit in sol-emn si-lence in a dull, dark dock, In a pes- ti - len-tial pris - on, with a
sit in sol-emn si-lence in a dull, dark dock, In a pes- ti - len-tial pris - on, with a

life - long lock, A - wait - ing the sen - sa - tion of a short, sharp shock, From a
life - long lock, A - wait - ing the sen - sa - tion of a short, sharp shock, From a
life - long lock, A - wait - ing the sen - sa - tion of a short, sharp shock, From a
cheap and chip - py chop - per on a big black block! A dull, dark dock, A
cheap and chip - py chop - per on a big black block! A dull, dark dock, A
cheap and chip - py chop - per on a big black block! A dull, dark dock, A
f
life - long lock, A short, sharp shock, A big black block! To
life - long lock, A short, sharp shock, A big black block! To
life - long lock, A short, sharp shock, A big black block! To

(Exeunt Pooh-Bah and Pish-Tush.)

Ko: This is simply appalling! I, who allowed myself to be respited at the last moment, simply in order to benefit my native town, am now required to die within a month, and that by a man whom I have loaded with honours! Is this public gratitude? Is this— *(Enter Nanki-Poo, with a rope in his hands.)* Go away, sir! How dare you? Am I never to be permitted to soliloquize?

Nanki: Oh, go on— don't mind me.

Ko: What are you going to do with that rope?

Nanki: I'm about to terminate an unendurable existence.

Ko: Terminate your existence? Oh, nonsense! What for?

Nanki: Because you are going to marry the girl I adore.

Ko: Nonsense, sir. I won't permit it. I am a humane man; and if you attempt anything of the kind, I shall order your instant arrest. Come, sir, desist at once, or I summon my guard.

Nanki: That's absurd. If you attempt to raise an alarm, I instantly perform the Happy Despatch with this dagger.

Ko: No, no, don't do that. This is horrible! *(Suddenly)* Why, you cold-blooded scoundrel, are you aware that, in taking your life, you are committing a crime which— which— which is— Oh! *(Struck by an idea)* Substitute!

Nanki: What's the matter?

Ko: Is it *absolutely certain* that you are resolved to die?

Nanki: Absolutely!

Ko: Will *nothing* shake your resolution?

Nanki: Nothing.

Ko: Threats, entreaties, prayers— all useless?

Nanki: All! My mind is made up.

Ko: Then, if you really mean what you say, and if you are absolutely resolved to die, and if nothing whatever will shake your determination— don't spoil yourself by committing suicide, but be beheaded handsomely at the hands of the Public Executioner!

Nanki: I don't see how that would benefit me.

Ko: You don't? Observe: you'll have a month to live, and you'll live like a fighting cock at my expense. When the day comes, there'll be a grand public ceremonial— you'll be the central figure— no one will attempt to deprive you of that distinction. There'll be a procession— bands— dead-march— bells tolling— all the girls in tears— Yum-Yum distracted— then, when it's all over, general rejoicings, and a display of fireworks in the evening. *You* won't see them, but they'll be there all the same.

Nanki: Do you think Yum-Yum would really be distracted at my death?

Ko: I am convinced of it. Bless you, she's the most tender-hearted little creature alive.

Nanki: I should be sorry to cause her pain. Perhaps, after all, if I were to withdraw from Japan, and travel in Europe for a couple of years, I might contrive to forget her.

Ko: Oh, I don't think you could forget Yum-Yum so easily; and, after all, what is more miserable than a love-blighted life?

Nanki: True.

Ko: Life without Yum-Yum— why, it seems absurd!

Nanki: And yet there are a good many people in the world who have to endure it.

Ko: Poor devils, yes! You are quite right not to be of their number.

Nanki: *(suddenly)* I *won't* be of their number!

Ko: Noble fellow!

Nanki: I'll tell you how we'll manage it. Let me marry Yum-Yum to-morrow, and in a month you may behead me.

Ko: No, no. I draw the line at Yum-Yum.

Nanki: Very good. If you can draw the line, so can I. *(Preparing rope)*

Ko: Stop, stop— listen one moment— be reasonable. How can I consent to your marrying Yum-Yum if I'm going to marry her myself?

Nanki: My good friend, she'll be a widow in a month, and you can marry her then.

Ko: That's true, of course. I quite see that. But, dear me! my position during the next month will be most unpleasant— most unpleasant.

Nanki: Not half so unpleasant as my position at the end of it.

Ko: But— dear me!— well— I agree— after all, it's only putting off my wedding for a month. But you won't prejudice her against me, will you? You see, I've educated her to be my wife; she's been taught to regard me as a wise and good man. Now I shouldn't like her views on that point disturbed.

Nanki: Trust me, she shall never learn the truth from me.

(Enter Chorus, Pooh-Bah, and Pish-Tush.)

No. 11. "With aspect stern and gloomy stride"

Finale of Act I

Ensemble

cide.
Don't hes-i - tate
cide.
Don't hes-i - tate
Your choice to name,
A dread-ful fate You'll suf-fer all the same,
Your choice to name,
A dread-ful fate You'll suf-fer all the same,
p
A dread-ful fate You'll suf-fer all the same.
A dread-ful fate You'll suf-fer all the same.
sf
p
f

Pooh-Bah
To ask you what you mean to do, we punc-tual-ly ap-pear.
Ko-Ko
Con-grat-u-late me, gen-tle-men, I've found a Vol-un-teer!
Chorus
The Jap-a-nese e-quiv-a-lent for
The Jap-a-nese e-quiv-a-lent for
Ko-Ko (presenting him)
'Tis Nan-ki-Poo! I think he'll do?
Hear, Hear, Hear! Hail, Nan-ki-Poo!
Hear, Hear, Hear! Hail, Nan-ki-Poo!

He yields his life if I'll Yum-Yum sur-ren-der; Now
Yes, yes, he'll do!
Yes, yes, he'll do!
p
I a-dore that girl with pas-sion ten-der, And could not yield her
p
with a read-y will, Or her al-lot, If I did not A-
dore my-self with pas - sion ten-d'rer still! With pas-sion ten-d'rer
colla voce

a tempo
(Enter Yum-Yum, Peep-Bo, and Pitti-Sing.)
still!
Ah, yes, He loves him-self with pas-sion ten - d'rer still!
rit.
Ah, yes, He loves him-self with pas-sion ten - d'rer still!
a tempo
rit.
Ko-Ko (to Nanki-Poo)
(Exit Ko-Ko.)
Take her— she's yours!
Allegro con brio (𝅗𝅥 = 132)
Yum-Yum
And bright - ly shines the dawn - ing
Nanki-Poo
The threat-ened cloud has passed a - way,

day; There's yet a month of af- ter-noon!
Peep-Bo
Then
Nanki-Poo
What tho' the night may come too soon, Then
Pooh-Bah and Pish-Tush
Then
Then let the throng Our joy ad - vance,
Then let the throng Our joy ad - vance,
Pitti-Sing
let the throng Our joy ad - vance, With laugh-ing
let the throng Our joy ad - vance, With laugh-ing
let the throng Our joy ad - vance, With laugh-ing

With laugh-ing song And mer-ry dance, Then let the throng Our joy ad-
With laugh-ing song And mer-ry dance,
song And mer - ry dance, Then let the throng Our joy ad-
song And mer - ry dance, Then let the throng Our joy ad-
song And mer - ry dance, Then let the throng Our joy ad-
vance, With laugh-ing song And mer-ry dance, With laugh-ing song And mer-ry
vance, With laugh-ing song And mer-ry dance, With laugh-ing song And mer-ry
vance, With laugh-ing song And mer-ry dance, With laugh-ing song And mer-ry
vance, With laugh-ing song And mer-ry dance, With laugh-ing song And mer-ry

Tutti
ff
dance, With laugh - ing song,
With
cre - - - scen - - - do ff
joy - ous shout, With joy - ous shout and ring - ing cheer, In - au - gu -

rate, in - au - gu - rate their brief ca - reer! With joy - ous
rate, in - au - gu - rate their brief ca - reer! With joy - ous shout and ring-ing
rate, in - au - gu - rate their brief ca - reer! With joy - ous shout and ring-ing
rate, in - au - gu - rate their brief ca - reer! With joy - ous shout and ring-ing
cheer, joy - - ous,
shout and ring - ing cheer, With
cheer, In - au - gu - rate their brief ca - reer! With joy - ous shout and ring-ing
cheer, In - au - gu - rate their brief ca - reer! With joy - ous shout and ring-ing
cheer, In - au - gu - rate their brief ca - reer! With joy - ous shout and ring-ing

1.

joy - - - - ous shout!

joy - ous, joy - ous shout!

cheer, In - au - gu - rate their brief ca - reer!

cheer, In - au - gu - rate their brief ca - reer!

cheer, In - au - gu - rate their brief ca - reer!

mf

Yum-Yum

Or far or near, or far or

Pitti-Sing

A day, a week, a month, a — year—

near,

Pitti-Sing

You'll live at least a hon - ey-moon! Then

Peep-Bo

Nanki-Poo

Then

Pooh-Bah

Life's e - ven - tide comes much too soon,

Pooh-Bah and Pish-Tush

Then

2.
shout! Laugh-ing song, mer - ry_ dance, with laugh-ing song and mer-ry_ dance.
reer, Laugh-ing song, mer - ry dance, with laugh-ing song and mer-ry dance.
reer, Laugh-ing song, mer - ry dance, with laugh-ing song and mer-ry dance.
reer, Laugh-ing song, mer - ry dance, with laugh-ing song and mer-ry dance.
Solo Pooh-Bah
As in a month you've got to die, If Ko-Ko tells us true, 'Twere
p
emp-ty com-pli-ment to cry, "Long life to Nan-ki - Poo!" But as one month you
poco rit.
a tempo
have to live As fel-low-cit - i - zen, This toast with three times three we'll give: "Long
cre - - scen - - do

p mf f

life, ——— long life to you, long life to you, long life —— to you-till

f p

Chorus

a tempo ff

May all good for-tune, all good for-tune pros-per you, May

ff

May all good for-tune, all good for-tune pros-per you, May

ff

May all good for-tune, all good for-tune pros-per you, May

ff

then!" May all good for-tune, all good for-tune pros-per you, May

(Exit Pooh-Bah.)

a tempo ff

you have health, may you have health and_ rich-es,_ too, May

you have health, may you have health and rich-es, too, May all good

you have health, may you have health and rich-es, too, May all good

you have health, may you have health and rich-es, too, May all good

do, in
you suc - ceed in all you do!
fortune prosper you, May you have health and riches, too, May you suc -
fortune prosper you, May you have health and riches, too, May you suc -
fortune prosper you, May you have health and riches, too, May you suc -
all, all you do!
Dance
Long life to you— till then!
ceed in all you do! Long life, long life to you—till then!
ceed in all you do! Long life, long life to you—till then!
ceed in all you do! Long life, long life to you—till then!
tr
tr

Allegro agitato ♩ = 76

(Enter Katisha, melodramatically.)

ff

Recit. Katisha

Your rev - els cease! As - sist me, all of you!

f a tempo

Why, who is

f

Why, who is

f a tempo

I

this whose e - vil eyes Rain blight on our fes - tiv - i - ties?

this whose e - vil eyes Rain blight on our fes - tiv - i - ties?

Recit.
claim my per-jured lov-er, Nan-ki-Poo!
Oh, fool! to shun de-
f
fp
lights — that nev-er cloy!
Recit.
Come back, oh, shal-low
Go, leave thy dead-ly work un-done!
Go, leave thy dead-ly work un-done!
f a tempo
fp
fool, come back to joy!
A-way! a-way! ill-fa-voured one!
A-way! a-way! ill-fa-voured one!
f a tempo
dim.

Nanki-Poo (aside to Yum-Yum)
(About to go)
Ah! 'Tis Ka-ti-sha, The maid of whom I told you.
p
Katisha (detaining him)
No! You shall not go, These arms shall thus en - fold you!
Allegro agitato
Katisha (addressing Nanki-Poo)
Oh fool, that flee-st My hal - lowed
f
p
joys! Oh blind, that see-st No e - qui-poise!
f
p

Oh rash, that judg-est From half, the whole!
Oh base, that grudg-est Love's light - est dole! Thy
heart un-bind, Oh fool, oh blind! Give me my place, Oh rash, oh base! Thy
heart un-bind, Give me my place, Oh fool, oh blind, Oh

rash, oh base! Thy heart_ un - bind,_ Give me, give me my
Tutti. Chorus
place. If she's thy bride, re- store her place, Oh fool, oh blind, oh rash, oh
f
Katisha (addressing Yum-Yum)
base! Pink cheek, that rul- est Where wis - dom
f
p
serves! Bright eye, that fool-est He- ro - ic nerves!
f
p

Rose lip, that scorn - est Lore - la - den years!
Smooth tongue, that warn - est Who right - ly hears! Thy
doom is nigh, Pink cheek, bright eye! Thy knell is rung, Rose lip, smooth tongue! Thy
doom is nigh, Thy knell is rung, Pink cheek, bright eye, Rose
p

lip, smooth tongue! Thy doom is nigh, Thy knell, thy knell is
rung.
Tutti. Chorus
If true her tale, thy knell is rung, Pink cheek, bright
If true her tale, thy knell is rung, Pink cheek, bright
f
accel.
Thy doom is
accel.
eye, rose lip, smooth tongue! If true her tale, thy knell is
eye, rose lip, smooth tongue! If true her tale, thy knell is
accel.
3
3
3
cresc.

nigh, Thy knell is rung, Thy knell, Thy
rung, If true her tale, thy knell is rung, Thy
rung, If true her tale, thy knell is rung, Thy
knell is rung!
knell is rung!
knell is rung!
Pitti-Sing
A-way, nor
pros-e-cute your quest– From our in-ten-tion, well ex-pressed, You can-not

turn us! The state of your con-nu-bial views To-wards the per-son you ac-
f
p
f
p
poco rit.
cuse Does not con - cern us!
poco rit.
Allegretto grazioso ♩.= 88
For ___ he's go-ing to mar-ry Yum-
p
Yum— Your an-ger pray bur-y, For all will be mer-ry, I
Chorus
Yum-Yum!
Yum-Yum!
think you had bet-ter suc-cumb— And join our ex-pres-sions of glee. On this
Cumb-cumb!
Cumb-cumb!

sub-ject I pray you be dumb– You'll find there are man-y Who'll
Dumb– dumb!
Dumb– dumb!
wed for a pen-ny–The word for your gui-dance is "Mum"– There's
Mum– mum!
Mum– mum!
lots of good fish in the sea! On this
Pitti-Sing with Soprano II
On this sub-ject we pray you be
On this sub-ject we pray you be

dumb—dumb—dumb. We think you had bet - ter suc - cumb—cumb—cumb! You'll
dumb—dumb—dumb. We think you had bet - ter suc - cumb—cumb—cumb! You'll
find there are man - y Who'll wed for a pen - ny, Who'll wed for a
find there are man - y Who'll wed for a pen - ny, Who'll wed for a
pen - ny—There are lots of good fish in the sea! There are
pen - ny—There are lots of good fish in the sea! There are

lots of good fish in the sea! There's lots of good fish, good fish in the
lots of good fish in the sea! There's lots of good fish, good fish in the
sf
sea! There's lots of good fish, good fish in the sea, in the sea, in the
sea! There's lots of good fish, good fish in the sea, in the sea, in the
sea, in the sea, in the sea!
sea, in the sea, in the sea!
sf
p
rall.

Andante ♩= 88 Katisha
The hour of glad- ness Is dead and gone; In si - lent
sad- ness I live a - lone! The hope I cher- ished All life - less
lies, And all has per - ished, all has per - ished Save
cresc.
cresc.
love, which nev - er dies, Which nev - er, nev - er
f
sempre f
f

Allegro agitato
Recit.
dies! Oh, faith - less one, this in - sult you shall
rue! In vain for mer - cy on your knees you'll
Allegro non troppo 𝅗𝅥 = 96
sue. I'll
tear the mask from your dis- guis - ing!
Nanki (aside)
Now comes the

Katisha
Nanki (aside)
blow! Pre - pare your-selves for news sur-pris- ing!
How foil my
foe?
Recit. Katisha
No min-strel he, de-spite bra - va - do!
a tempo
Yum-Yum (aside, struck by an idea)
Ha! ha! I know!
fp
Recit. Katisha
He is the son of your—
meno mosso
Nanki-Poo, Yum-Yum, and Chorus (interrupting, to drown her voice)
ff
O ni! bik - ku - ri shak - ku - ri to!
Recit. Katisha
In vain you in - ter -

rupt with this tor - na - do! He is the on - ly son of your—
unison
O ni!
ff
I'll spoil—
bik - ku - ri shak - ku - ri to!
O ni! bik - ku - ri shak - ku - ri
—your gay gam - ba - do! He is the son—
to!
O ni! bik - ku - ri shak - ku - ri

— of your —
— the son of your —
to! O ni! bik - ku - ri shak - ku - ri to!
O ni! bik - ku - ri shak - ku - ri to! O - ya, O -
rall.
Allegro con brio 𝅗𝅥 = 132
Katisha
ya! Ye tor - rents roar! Ye tem - pests howl! Your wrath out -
pour With an - gry growl! Do ye your worst, my ven - geance - call Shall rise tri -
f

Tutti
um - phant o - ver all! We'll hear no more, Ill - o - mened owl, To joy we
più f
soar, De-spite your scowl; The ech - oes of our fes - ti - val Shall rise tri -
Katisha
um - phant o - ver all! Pre - pare for woe, Ye
meno f
haugh - ty lords, At once I go Mi -

Tutti
ka - do - wards. A - way you_ go, Col -
più f
lect_ your_ hordes; Pro - claim your woe In
Yum-Yum
dis - mal_ chords. We do not heed their
p
Nanki-Poo
dis - mal_ sound. For joy reigns ev - 'ry -

Yum-Yum

where a - round. We do not heed their dis - mal

sound. For joy reigns ev - 'ry-where a - round. The *p* ech - oes

Nanki-Poo

For joy reigns ev - 'ry - where a - round. The *p* ech - oes

Chorus *p*

We'll hear no

p

We'll hear no

pp

of— our fes - ti - val Shall rise tri - um - phant o - ver all!

of— our fes - ti - val Shall rise tri - um - phant o - ver all! Shall

more, Ill - o - mened owl, To joy we soar, De-spite your scowl!

more, Ill - o - mened owl, To joy we soar, De-spite your scowl!

Shall rise_ tri - um - - - phant, Tri - um - phant
rise tri - um - - - phant o - ver all! Tri - um - phant
To
To
cresc.
f
f
f
Katisha
o - ver all! Shall rise tri - um - phant o - ver all! My
o - ver all! Shall rise tri - um - phant o - ver all!
joy___ we soar, To joy we soar, De - spite your scowl!
joy___ we soar, To joy we soar, De - spite your scowl!

wrongs with ven - geance shall be crowned!
ff
We do not heed their
ff
We do not heed their
cresc.
ff
dis - mal sound, For joy reigns ev - 'ry - where a - round! We
dis - mal sound, For joy reigns ev - 'ry-where a - round! We
do not heed their dis - mal sound, For joy reigns ev - 'ry - where a -
do not heed their dis - mal sound, For joy reigns ev - 'ry-where a -

Katisha

My wrongs with ven - geance shall be crowned, My

round! We do not heed their dis - mal sound, For

round! We do not heed their dis - mal sound, For

wrongs with ven - - - geance shall — be crowned!

joy reigns ev - - - 'ry - where — a - round! —

joy reigns ev - - - 'ry - where — a - round! —

con forza

ff

(Katisha rushes furiously up-stage, clearing the crowd away right and left, finishing on steps at the back of stage.)

End of Act I

ACT II

Scene: *Ko-Ko's Garden. Yum-Yum discovered seated at her boudoir table, surrounded by maidens, who are dressing her hair and painting her face and lips, as she judges the effect in a mirror.*

No. 12. "Braid the raven hair"

Opening Chorus and Solo

Pitti-Sing and Girls

Chorus
SOPRANO I
Braid the ra - ven
SOPRANO II
Braid the ra - ven
hair–Weave the sup - ple tress–
Deck the maid - en fair In her
love - li - ness–
Paint the pret - ty face–Dye the cor - al lip–

Em - pha-size the grace Of her la - dy - ship! Art and na - ture,
Em - pha-size the grace Of her la - dy - ship! Art and na - ture,
thus al - lied, Go to make a pret-ty bride, Art and na-ture, thus al-
thus al - lied, Go to make a pret - ty bride, Art and na-ture, thus al-
lied, Go to make a pret - ty bride.
lied, Go to make a pret - ty bride.
f

Pitti-Sing
Sit with down-cast eye— Let it brim with dew— Try if you can
cry— We will do so, too. When you're sum-moned, start
Like a fright-ened roe— Flut-ter, lit-tle heart,
Col-our, come and go! Mod-es - ty at mar-riage - tide

Well be - comes a pret-ty bride, Mod-es - ty at mar-riage-tide Well be-
p
comes a pret - ty bride.
f
f
Braid the ra-ven hair—Weave the sup - ple tress— Deck the maid-en fair In her
f
Braid the ra-ven hair—Weave the sup - ple tress— Deck the maid-en fair In her
f
love - li - ness— Paint the pret-ty face— Dye the cor - al lip—
love - li - ness— Paint the pret-ty face— Dye the cor - al lip—

(Exeunt Pitti-Sing, Peep-Bo, and Chorus.)

Yum: Yes, I am indeed beautiful! Sometimes I sit and wonder, in my artless Japanese way, why it is that I am so much more attractive than anybody else in the whole world. Can this be vanity? No! Nature is lovely and rejoices in her loveliness. I am a child of Nature, and take after my mother.

No. 13. "The sun, whose rays are all ablaze"

Song

Yum-Yum

Andante comodo (♩= 66)
mf
p sostenuto
The sun, whose rays Are all a-blaze With ev-er-liv-ing glo-ry,
Does not de-ny His maj-es-ty— He scorns to tell a sto-ry!
He won't ex-claim, "I blush for shame, So kind-ly be in-dul-gent,"

But, fierce and bold, In fier-y gold, He glo-ries all ef-ful-gent. I
mean to rule the earth, — As he the sky— We real-ly know our worth, —
cresc.
— The sun and I! I mean to rule the earth, As he the sky— We
dim.
rall.
a tempo
real-ly know our worth, The sun and I!
a tempo
rall.
mf
p sostenuto

Ob-serve his flame, That plac- id dame, The moon's Ce - les - tial High - ness;
There's not a trace Up - on her face Of dif - fi - dence or shy - ness:
She bor-rows light That, thro' the night, Man-kind may all ac - claim her!
And, truth to tell, She lights up well; So I, for one, don't blame her.

(Enter Pitti-Sing and Peep-Bo.)

Yum: Yes, everything seems to smile upon me. I am to be married to-day to the man I love best, and I believe I am the very happiest girl in Japan!

Peep: The happiest girl indeed, for she is indeed to be envied who has attained happiness in all but perfection.

Yum: In "all but" perfection?

Peep: Well, dear, it can't be denied that the fact that your husband is to be beheaded in a month is, in its way, a drawback. It does seem to take the top off it, you know.

Pitti: I don't know about that. It all depends!

Peep: At all events, *he* will find it a drawback.

Pitti: Not necessarily. Bless you, it all depends!

Yum: *(in tears)* I think it very indelicate of you to refer to such a subject on such a day. If my married happines *is* to be— to be—

Peep. Cut short.

Yum: Well, cut short— in a month, can't you let me forget it? *(Weeping)*

(Enter Nanki-Poo, followed by Pish-Tush.)

Nanki: Yum-Yum in tears— and on her wedding-morn!

Yum: *(sobbing)* They've been reminding me that in a month you're to be beheaded! *(Bursts into tears)*

Pitti: Yes, we've been reminding her that you're to be beheaded. *(Bursts into tears)*

Peep: It's quite true, you know, you *are* to be beheaded! *(Bursts into tears)*

Nanki: *(aside)* Humph! Now some bridegrooms would be depressed by this sort of thing! *(Aloud)* A month? Well, what's a month? Bah! These divisions of time are purely arbitrary. Who says twenty-four hours make a day?

Pitti: There's a popular impression to that effect.

Nanki: Then we'll efface it. We'll call each second a minute— each minute an hour— each hour a day— and each day a year. At that rate we've about thirty years of married happiness before us!

Peep: And, at that rate, this interview has already lasted four hours and three-quarters! *(Exit Peep-Bo.)*

Yum: *(still sobbing)* Yes. How time flies when one is thoroughly enjoying oneself!

Nanki: That's the way to look at it! Don't let's be downhearted! There's a silver lining to every cloud.

Yum: Certainly. Let's— let's be perfectly happy! *(Almost in tears)*

Pish: By all means. Let's— let's thoroughly enjoy ourselves.

Pitti: It's— it's absurd to cry! *(Trying to force a laugh)*

Yum: Quite ridiculous! *(Trying to laugh)*

(All break into a forced and melancholy laugh.)

No. 14. "Brightly dawns our wedding day"

Madrigal

Yum-Yum, Pitti-Sing, Nanki-Poo, and Pish-Tush

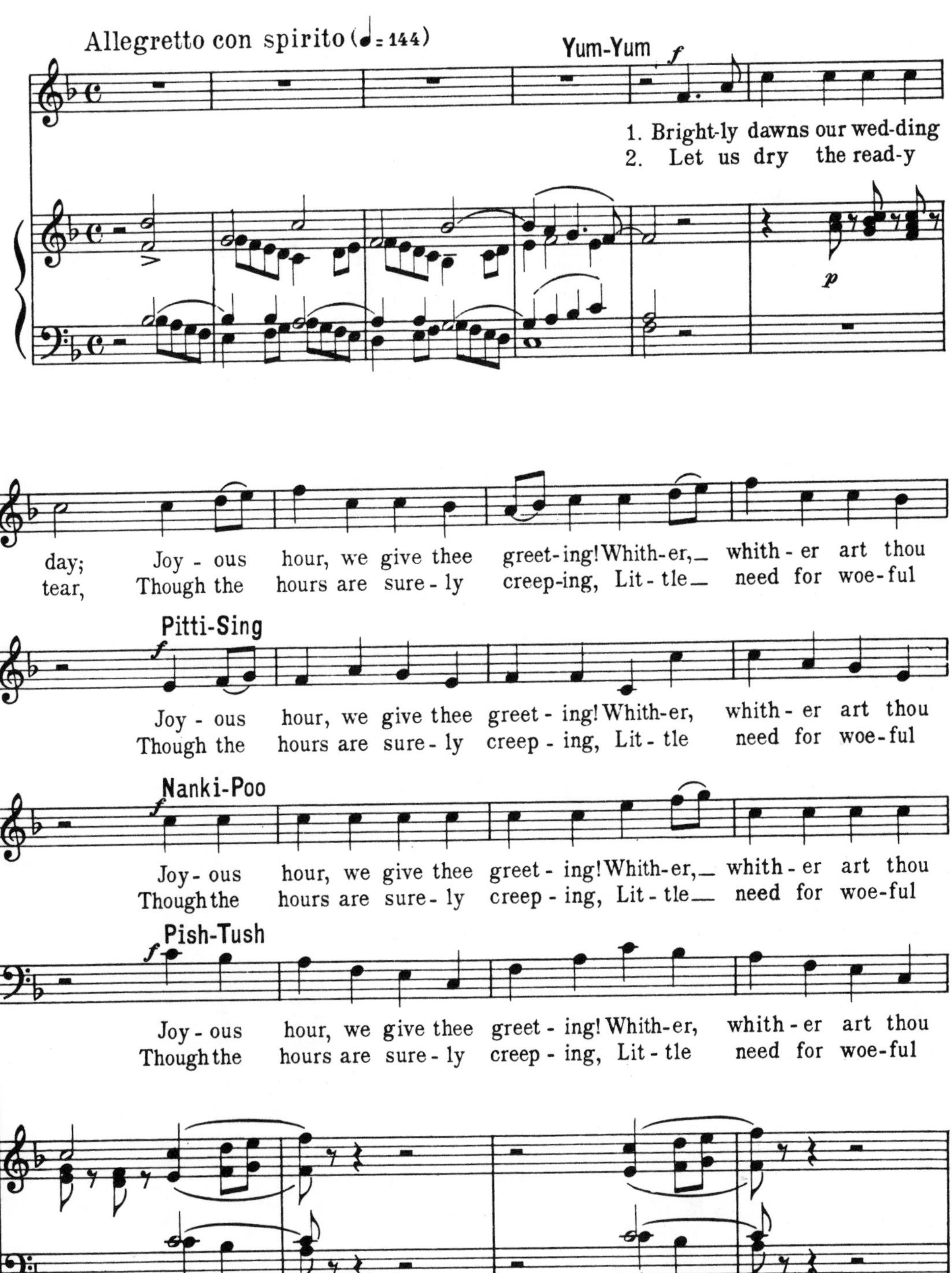

fleet - ing? Fick - le moment, prith - ee stay! Fick - le mo - ment, prith - ee
weep - ing, Till the sad sun-down is near, Till the sad sun-down is
fleet - ing? Fick - le mo-ment, prith - ee stay! Fick - le mo - ment, prith - ee
weep - ing, Till the sad sun-down is near, Till the sad sun-down is
fleet - ing? Fick - le mo-ment, prith - ee stay! Fick - le mo - ment, prith - ee
weep - ing, Till the sad sun-down is near, Till the sad sun-down is
fleet - ing? Fick - le mo-ment, prith - ee stay! Fick - le mo - ment, prith - ee
weep - ing, Till the sad sun-down is near, Till the sad sun-down is
stay!
near.
stay!
near.
Plea-sures
I to-
stay!
near.
stay!
near.
What though mor-tal joys be hol-low?
All must sip the cup of sor-row—
Ped.

Though the toc-sin sound, ere long, Though
This the close of ev-'ry song, This —

come, if sor-rows fol-low: Though the toc-sin sound, ere long, Ding
day, and thou to-mor-row This the close of ev-'ry song, Ding

Though the toc-sin sound, ere long, ere long,
This the close of ev-'ry, ev-'ry song,

Though the toc-sin sound, ere long, Ding
This the close of ev-'ry song, Ding

— the toc-sin sound, ere long, Though — the toc-sin sound, ere — long, Ding
— the close of ev-'ry song, This — the close of ev-'ry — song, Ding

dong! Ding dong! Ding dong! Ding dong! Ding

Though the — toc-sin sound, ere — long, sound, ere long,
This the — close of ev-'ry — song, this the close,

dong! Ding dong! Ding dong! Ding dong! Ding

— dong! Ding — dong! Yet un - til the shad - ows fall O - ver
— dong! Ding — dong! What though sol - emn shad - ows fall, Soon - er,
— dong! Ding — dong! Yet un - til the shad - ows fall O - ver
— dong! Ding — dong! What though sol - emn shad - ows fall, Soon - er,
Ding dong! Ding dong! Yet un - til the shad - ows fall O - ver
Ding dong! Ding dong! What though sol - emn shad - ows fall, Soon - er,
— dong! Ding — dong! Yet un - til the shad - ows fall O - ver
— dong! Ding — dong! What though sol - emn shad - ows fall, Soon - er,
one and o - ver all,
lat - er, o - ver all, Sing a mer - ry mad - ri - gal, Sing a — mer - ry mad - ri -
one and o - ver all,
lat - er, o - ver all,
Sing a — mer - ry mad - ri -
one and o - ver all,
lat - er, o - ver all,
Sing a mer - ry mad - ri -
one and o - ver all,
lat - er, o - ver all,
Sing a mer - ry mad - ri -

gal, Sing a mer-ry mad-ri - gal: Fa la, Fa
gal, Sing a mer-ry mad-ri - gal: Fa la la la la la, Fa la
gal, Sing a mer-ry mad-ri - gal: Fa la la
gal, Sing a mer-ry mad-ri - gal: Fa la la la la, Fa la la la la la
ff
la, Fa la la la la, Fa la la la la, Fa
la la la la la, Fa la la, Fa la, Fa la,
la la, Fa la la la la, Fa la la la
la, Fa la la la la la la, Fa

(Exeunt Pitti-Sing and Pish-Tush.)

(Nanki-Poo embraces Yum-Yum. Enter Ko-Ko. Nanki-Poo releases Yum-Yum.)

Ko: Go on— don't mind me.

Nanki: I'm afraid we're distressing you.

Ko: Never mind, I must get used to it. Only please do it by degrees. Begin by putting your arm around her waist. *(Nanki-Poo does so.)* There! let me get used to that first.

Yum: Oh, wouldn't you like to retire? It must pain you to see us so affectionate together!

Ko: No, I must learn to bear it! Now oblige me by allowing her head to rest on your shoulder.

Nanki: Like that? *(He does so. Ko-Ko is much affected.)*

Ko: I am much obliged to you. Now— kiss her! *(He does so. Ko-Ko writhes with anguish.)* Thank you— it's simple torture!

Yum: Come, come, bear up. After all, it's only for a month.

Ko: No. It's no use deluding oneself with false hopes.

Nanki and Yum: What do you mean?

Ko: *(to Yum-Yum)* My child— my poor child! *(Aside)* How shall I break it to her? *(Aloud)* My little bride that was to have been—

Yum: *(delighted)* *Was* to have been?

Ko: Yes, you never can be mine!

Nanki: } *(in ecstasy)* { What!
Yum: } { I'm so glad!

Ko: I've just ascertained that, by the Mikado's law, when a married man is beheaded his wife is buried alive.

Nanki and Yum: Buried alive!

Ko: Buried alive. It's a most unpleasant death.

Nanki: But whom did you get that from?

Ko: Oh, from Pooh-Bah. He's my solicitor.

Yum: But he may be mistaken!

Ko: So I thought; so I consulted the Attorney-General, the Lord Chief Justice, the Master of the Rolls, the Judge Ordinary, and the Lord Chancellor. They're all of the same opinion. Never knew such unanimity on a point of law in my life!

Nanki: But stop a bit! This law has never been put in force.

Ko: Not yet. You see, flirting is the only crime punishable with decapitation, and married men never flirt.

Nanki: Of course, they don't. I quite forgot that! Well, I suppose I may take it that my dream of happiness is at an end!

Yum: Darling— I don't want to appear selfish, and I love you with all my heart— I don't suppose I shall ever love anybody else half as much— but when I agreed to marry you— my own— I had no idea— pet— that I should have to be buried alive in a month!

Nanki: Nor I! It's the very first I've heard of it!

Yum: It— it makes a difference, doesn't it?

Nanki: It *does* make a difference, of course.

Yum: You see— burial alive— it's such a stuffy death.

Nanki: I call it a beast of a death.

Yum: You see my difficulty, don't you?

Nanki: Yes, and I see my own. If I insist on your carrying out your promise, I doom you to a hideous death; if I release you, you marry Ko-Ko at once.

No. 15. "Here's a how-de-do!"

Trio

Yum-Yum, Nanki-Poo, and Ko-Ko

Nanki-Poo
Here's a pret - ty mess! In a month, or
cresc.
p
less, I must die with-out a wed-ding! Let the bit-ter tears I'm shed-ding
Wit-ness my dis-tress, Here's a pret - ty mess! Here's a pret - ty
Ko-Ko
mess! Here's a state of things! To her life she clings!

Mat-ri-mo-ni - al de-vo-tion Does-n't seem to suit her no-tion—
Bur-i - al it brings! Here's a state of things! Here's a state of
Yum-Yum
With a pas - sion that's in -
Nanki-Poo
With a pas - sion that's in -
things! With a pas - sion that's in -

tense I wor-ship and a - dore, But the laws of com-mon
tense I wor-ship and a - dore, But the laws of com-mon
tense You wor-ship and a - dore, But the laws of com-mon
sense We ought-n't to — ig - nore. If what he says is true, 'Tis
sense We ought-n't to — ig - nore. If what he says is true, 'Tis
sense You ought-n't to ig - nore. If what I say is true, 'Tis
death to mar-ry you! Here's a pret-ty state of things!
death to mar-ry you! Here's a pret-ty state of things!
death to mar-ry you! Here's a pret-ty state of things!

cresc.
Here's a pret-ty how-de-do! Here's a pret-ty state of things! a
cresc.
Here's a pret-ty how-de-do! Here's a pret-ty state of things! a
cresc.
Here's a pret-ty how-de-do! Here's a pret-ty state of things! a
cresc.
f
pret-ty state of things! Here's a how-de-do!
f
pret-ty state of things! Here's a how-de-do!
pret-ty state of things! Here's a how-de-
For if what he says is true, I can-not, can-not mar-ry you!
For if what he says is true, I can-not, can-not mar-ry you!
do! For if what he says is true, He can-not, can-not mar-ry you!

(Exit Yum-Yum.)

Ko: *(going up to Nanki-Poo)* My poor boy, I'm really very sorry for you.

Nanki: Thanks, old fellow. I'm sure you are.

Ko: You see I'm quite helpless.

Nanki: I quite see that.

Ko: I can't conceive anything more distressing than to have one's marriage broken off at the last moment. But you shan't be disappointed of a wedding— you shall come to mine.

Nanki: It's awfully kind of you, but that's impossible.

Ko: Why so?

Nanki: To-day I die.

Ko: What do you mean?

Nanki: I can't live without Yum-Yum. This afternoon I perform the Happy Despatch.

Ko: No, no— pardon me— I can't allow that.

Nanki: Why not?

Ko: Why, hang it all, you're under contract to die by the hand of the Public Executioner in a month's time! If you kill yourself, what's to become of me? Why, I shall have to be executed in your place!

Nanki: It would certainly seem so!

(Enter Pooh-Bah.)

Ko: Now then, Lord Mayor, what is it?

Pooh: The Mikado and his suite are approaching the city, and will be here in ten minutes.

Ko: The Mikado! He's coming to see whether his orders have been carried out! *(To Nanki-Poo)* Now look here, you know— this is getting serious— a bargain's a bargain, and you really mustn't frustrate the ends of justice by committing suicide. As a man of honour and a gentleman, you are bound to die ignominiously by the hands of the Public Executioner.

Nanki: Very well, then— behead me.

Ko: What, now?

Nanki: Certainly; at once.

Pooh: Chop it off! Chop it off!

Ko: My good sir, I don't go about prepared to execute gentlemen at a moment's notice. Why, I never even killed a blue-bottle!

Pooh: Still, as Lord High Executioner—

Ko: My good sir, as Lord High Executioner I've got to behead him in a month. I'm not ready yet. I don't know how it's done. I'm going to take lessons. I mean to begin with a guinea pig, and work my way through the animal kingdom till I come to a Second Trombone. Why, you don't suppose that, as a humane man, I'd have accepted the post of Lord High Executioner if I hadn't thought the duties purely nominal? I *can't* kill you— I can't kill anything! I can't kill anybody! *(Weeps)*

Nanki: Come, my poor fellow, we all have unpleasant duties to discharge at times; after all, what is it? If I don't mind, why should you? Remember, sooner or later it must be done.

Ko: *(springing up suddenly) Must it?* I'm not so sure about that!

Nanki: What do you mean?

Ko: Why should I kill you when making an affidavit that you've been executed will do just as well? Here are plenty of witnesses— the Lord Chief Justice, Lord High Admiral, Commander-in-Chief, Secretary of State for the Home Department, First Lord of the Treasury, and Chief Commissioner of Police.

Nanki: But where are they?

Ko: There they are. They'll all swear to it— won't you? *(To Pooh-Bah)*

Pooh: Am I to understand that all of us high Officers of State are required to perjure ourselves to ensure your safety!

Ko: Why not? You'll be grossly insulted, as usual.

Pooh: Will the insult be cash down, or at a date?

Ko: It will be a ready-money transaction.

Pooh: *(aside)* Well, it will be a useful discipline. *(Aloud)* Very good. Choose your fiction, and I'll endorse it! *(Aside)* Ha! ha! Family Pride, how do you like *that*, my buck?

Nanki: But I tell you that life without Yum-Yum—

Ko: Oh, Yum-Yum, Yum-Yum! Bother Yum-Yum! Here, Commissionaire *(to Pooh Bah)*, go and fetch Yum-Yum. *(Exit Pooh-Bah.)* Take Yum-Yum and marry Yum-Yum, only go away and never come back again. *(Enter Pooh-Bah with Yum-Yum.)* Here she is. Yum-Yum, are you particularly busy?

Yum: Not particularly.

Ko: You've five minutes to spare?

Yum: Yes.

Ko: Then go along with his Grace the Archbishop of Titipu; he'll marry you at once.

Yum: But if I'm to be buried alive?

Ko: Now, don't ask any questions, but do as I tell you, and Nanki-Poo will explain all.

Nanki: But one moment—

Ko: Not for worlds. Here comes the Mikado, no doubt to ascertain whether I've obeyed his decree; and if he finds you alive I shall have the greatest difficulty in persuading him that I've beheaded you. *(Exeunt Nanki-Poo and Yum-Yum, followed by Pooh-Bah.)* Close thing that, for here he comes! *(Exit Ko-Ko. Enter procession, heralding Mikado, with Katisha.)*

No. 16. "Mi-ya sa-ma"

March of the Mikado's Troops, Chorus, and Duet

Mikado, Katisha, Girls, and Men

Begin on cue "don't ask" etc.

Allegro moderato ♩= 152

pp *(Dialogue continues)*

Enter Chorus, etc.

f

Girls
f
Mi - ya sa - ma, mi - ya sa - ma, On n'm-ma no ma - yé ni Pi - ra Pi - ra
Men
f
Mi - ya sa - ma, mi - ya sa - ma, On n'm-ma no ma - yé ni Pi - ra Pi - ra
f
su - ru no wa Nan gia — na —— To - ko ton - ya - ré ton - ya - ré
su - ru no wa Nan gia — na —— To - ko ton - ya - ré ton - ya - ré
na!
na!

Mi - ya sa - ma, mi - ya sa - ma, On n'm-ma no ma - yé ni Pi - ra Pi - ra
Mi - ya sa - ma, mi - ya sa - ma, On n'm-ma no ma - yé ni Pi - ra Pi - ra
su - ru no wa Nan gia _ na ___ To - ko ton - ya - ré ton - ya - ré
su - ru no wa Nan gia _ na ___ To - ko ton - ya - ré ton - ya - ré
na!
na!
f

Mikado
From ev-'ry kind of man O - be-dience
I ___ ex - pect; I'm the Em-p'ror of Ja - pan—
Katisha
And I'm his daugh-ter - in - law e - lect! He'll mar-ry his son (He's on- ly got one) To his daugh-ter - in - law e - lect.
Mikado
My— mor-als have been de - clared Par-tic - u -
p

Katisha
lar - ly cor - rect; But they're noth-ing at all, com-pared With those of his
daugh-ter - in-law e - lect. Bow— Bow— To his daugh-ter- in-law e - lect.
Chorus
f
Bow— Bow— To his daugh-ter - in - law e - lect.
f
Bow— Bow— To his daugh-ter - in - law e - lect.
f
dim.
Mikado
In a
p
dim.
r. h.

fa-ther-ly kind of way I gov-ern each tribe_ and sect, All
Katisha
Ex-cept his daugh-ter-in-law e-lect! As
cheer-ful-ly own my sway—
tough as a bone, With a will of her own, Is his daugh-ter-in-law e-
Mikado
Katisha
lect. My na-ture is love and light—My free-dom from all_ de-fect— Is

Attacca No. 17

No. 17. "A more humane Mikado"

Solo and Chorus

Mikado, Girls, and Men

is my ver-y hu - mane en-deav-our To make, to some ex - tent,— Each
p
rall.
a tempo
e - vil liv-er A run-ning riv-er Of harm-less mer - ri - ment. My
rall.
a tempo
ob - ject all sub - lime I shall a-chieve in time— To
let the pun-ish-ment fit the crime, The pun-ish-ment fit the crime; And

make each pris - 'ner pent Un - will - ing - ly rep - re - sent A

source of in - no - cent mer - ri - ment, Of in - no - cent mer - ri - ment!

p

All

pros - y dull so - ci - e - ty sin - ners, Who chat - ter and bleat and

ad - ver - tis - ing quack who wea - ries With tales of count - less

bore, Are sent to hear ser-mons From mys-ti-cal Ger-mans Who
cures, His teeth, I've en-act-ed, Shall all be ex-tract-ed By
preach from ten till four. The am-a-teur ten-or, whose vo-cal vil-lain-ies
ter-ri-fied am-a-teurs. The mu-sic-hall sing-er at-tends a se-ries Of
All de-sire to shirk, Shall, dur-ing off-hours, Ex-hib-it his powers To
mass-es and fugues and "ops" By Bach, in-ter-wov-en With Spohr and Beethoven, At
Madame Tus-saud's wax-work. The la-dy who dyes a chem-i-cal yel-low, Or
clas-si-cal Mon-day Pops. The bil-liard sharp whom an-y-one catch-es, His

stains her grey hair puce, Or pinches her fig-ger, Is blacked like a nig-ger With
doom's ex-treme-ly hard— He's made to dwell In a dun - geon cell On a
per-ma-nent wal-nut juice. The id - iot who, in rail - way car - ria-ges,
spot that's al - ways barred. And there he plays ex - trav-a-gant match-es In
Scrib-bles on win-dow-panes, We on - ly suf - fer To ride on a buf - fer In
fit - less fin - ger-stalls, On a cloth un-true, With a twist - ed cue And el-
rall.
a tempo
Par - lia - men - t'ry trains.
lip - ti - cal bil - liard balls.
My ob - ject all sub-lime I
a tempo
rall.
pp

shall a-chieve in time— To let the pun-ish-ment fit the crime, The

pun-ish-ment fit the crime; And make each pris-'ner pent Un-

will-ing-ly rep-re-sent A source of in-no-cent mer-ri-ment, Of

in-no-cent mer-ri-ment!

Chorus

His ob-ject all sub-lime He

His ob-ject all sub-lime He

ff

will a-chieve in time— To let the pun-ish-ment fit the crime, The
will a-chieve in time— To let the pun-ish-ment fit the crime, The
pun-ish-ment fit the crime; And make each pris-'ner pent Un-
pun-ish-ment fit the crime; And make each pris-'ner pent Un-
will-ing-ly rep-re-sent A source of in-no-cent
will-ing-ly rep-re-sent A source of in-no-cent

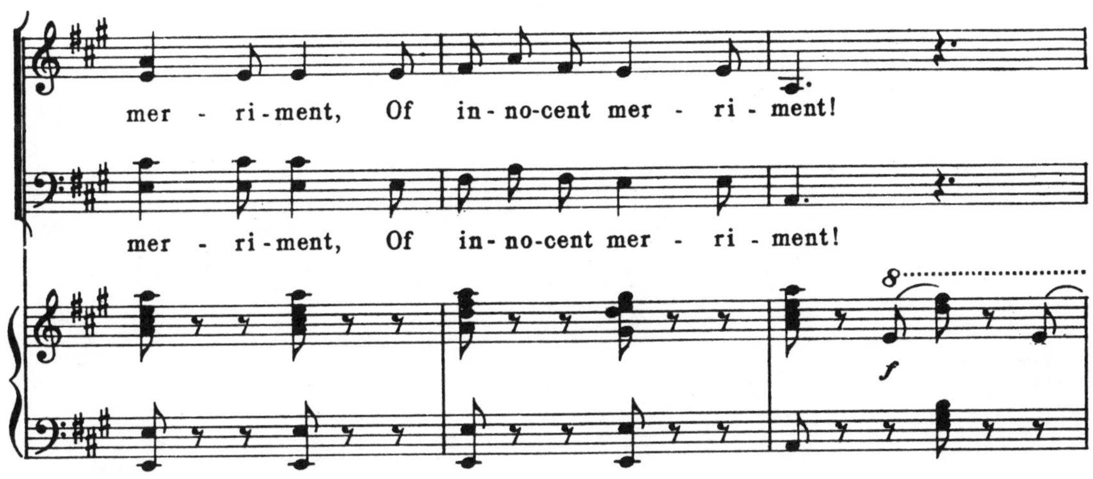

(Enter Pooh-Bah, Ko-Ko, and Pitti-Sing. All kneel. Pooh-Bah hands a paper to Ko-Ko.)

Ko: I am honoured in being permitted to welcome your Majesty. I guess the object of your Majesty's visit— your wishes have been attended to. The execution has taken place.

Mik: Oh, you've had an execution, have you?

Ko: Yes. The Coroner has just handed me his certificate.

Pooh: I am the Coroner. *(Ko-Ko hands certificate to Mikado.)*

Mik: And this is the certificate of his death. *(Reads)* "At Titipu, in the presence of the Lord Chancellor, Lord Chief Justice, Attorney General, Secretary of State for the Home Department, Lord Mayor, and Groom of the Second Floor Front—"

Pooh: They were all present, your Majesty. I counted them myself.

Mik: Very good house. I wish I'd been in time for the performance.

Ko: A tough fellow he was, too— a man of gigantic strength. His struggles were terrific. It was really a remarkable scene.

Mik: Describe it.

No. 18. "The criminal cried as he dropped him down"

Trio and Chorus

Ko-Ko, Pitti-Sing, Pooh-Bah, Girls, and Men

squirmed and strug-gled, And gur-gled and gug-gled, I drew my snick-er-
snee, my snick-er - snee! Oh, nev-er shall I For-
get the cry, Or the shriek that shriek-ed he, As I
gnashed my teeth, When from its sheath I drew my snick-er - snee!
Tutti & Chorus
f
We
f
We

know him well, He can-not tell Un-true or ground-less tales— He
know him well, He can-not tell Un-true or ground-less tales— He
al-ways tries To ut-ter lies, And ev-'ry time he fails.
al-ways tries To ut-ter lies, And ev-'ry time he fails.
Pitti-Sing
2. He shiv-ered and shook as he gave the sign For the stroke he did-n't deserve; When all of a sud-den his eye met mine, And it

seemed to brace his nerve; For he nod-ded his head and kissed his hand, And he
whis-tled an air, did he, As the sa - bre true Cut clean - ly through His
cer-vi-cal ver-te - bræ, his ver-te - bræ! When a
man's a-fraid, A beau-ti-ful maid Is a cheer-ing sight to see; And it's

oh, I'm glad That mo-ment sad Was soothed by sight of me!
Chorus
f
Her
f
Her
ter-ri-ble tale You can't as-sail, With truth it quite a - grees; Her
ter-ri-ble tale You can't as-sail, With truth it quite a - grees; Her
f
taste ex-act For fault-less fact A - mounts to a dis-ease.
rit.
taste ex-act For fault - less fact A - mounts to a dis-ease.
rit.
rit.

Pooh-Bah
3. Now tho' you'd have said that head was dead (For its own-er dead was he), It
a tempo
p
stood on its neck, with a smile well-bred, And bowed three times to me! — It was
none of your im-pu-dent off-hand nods, But as hum-ble as could be; For it
clear-ly knew The def-er-ence due To a man of ped-i-gree, —

of ped-i - gree! And it's oh, I vow, This death - ly bow Was a
touch - ing sight to see; Though trunk - less, yet It
could - n't for - get The def - er - ence due to me!
Chorus
This
This
haugh - ty youth, He speaks the truth When - ev - er he finds it pays; And
haugh - ty youth, He speaks the truth When - ev - er he finds it pays; And

(Exeunt Chorus.)

Mik: All this is very interesting, and I should like to have seen it. But we came about a totally different matter. A year ago my son, the heir to the throne of Japan, bolted from our Imperial Court.

Ko: Indeed! Had he any reason to be dissatisfied with his position?

Kat: None whatever. On the contrary, I was going to marry him— yet he fled!

Pooh: I am surprised that he should have fled from one so lovely!

Kat: That's not true.

Pooh: No!

Kat: You hold that I am not beautiful because my face is plain. But you know nothing; you are still unenlightened. Learn, then, that it is not in the face alone that beauty is to be sought. My face is unattractive!

Pooh: It is.

Kat: But I have a left shoulder-blade that is a miracle of loveliness. People come miles to see it. My right elbow has a fascination that few can resist.

Pooh: Allow me!

Kat: It is on view Tuesdays and Fridays, on presentation of visiting card. As for my circulation, it is the largest in the world.

Ko: And yet he fled!

Mik: And is now masquerading in this town, disguised as a Second Trombone.

Ko, Pooh, and Pitti: A Second Trombone!

Mik: Yes; would it be troubling you too much if I asked you to produce him? He goes by the name of—

Kat: Nanki-Poo.

Mik: Nanki-Poo.

Ko: It's quite easy— that is, it's rather difficult. In point of fact, he's gone abroad!

Mik: Gone abroad? His address!

Ko: Knightsbridge!

Kat: *(who is reading certificate of death)* Ha!

Mik: What's the matter?

Kat: See here— his name— Nanki-Poo— beheaded this morning. Oh, where shall I find another! Where shall I find another!

(Ko-Ko, Pooh-Bah, and Pitti-Sing fall on their knees.)

Mik: *(looking at paper)* Dear, dear, dear! this is very tiresome. *(To Ko-Ko)* My poor fellow, in your anxiety to carry out my wishes you have beheaded the heir to the throne of Japan!

Ko: I beg to offer an unqualified apology.

Pooh: I desire to associate myself with that expression of regret.

Pitti: We really hadn't the least notion—

Mik: Of course you hadn't. How could you? Come, come, my good fellow, don't distress yourself— it was no fault of yours. If a man of exalted rank chooses to disguise himself as a Second Trombone, he must take the consequences. It really distresses me to see you take on so. I've no doubt he thoroughly deserved all he got. *(They rise.)*

Ko: We are infinitely obliged to your Majesty—

Pitti: Much obliged, your Majesty.

Pooh: Very much obliged, your Majesty.

Mik: Obliged? not a bit. Don't mention it. How *could* you tell?

Pooh: No, of course we couldn't tell who the gentleman really was.

Pitti: It wasn't written on his forehead, you know.

Ko: It might have been on his pocket-handkerchief, but Japanese don't use pocket-handkerchiefs! Ha! ha! ha!

Mik: Ha! ha! ha! *(To Katisha)* I forget the punishment for compassing the death of the Heir Apparent.

Ko, Pooh, and Pitti: Punishment! *(They drop down on their knees again.)*

Mik: Yes. Something lingering, with boiling oil in it, I fancy. Something of that sort. I think boiling oil occurs in it, but I'm not sure. I know it's something humorous, but lingering, with either boiling oil or melted lead. Come, come, don't fret— I'm not a bit angry.

Ko: *(in abject terror)* If your Majesty will accept our assurance, we had no idea—

Mik: Of course—

Pitti: I knew nothing about it.

Pooh: I wasn't there.

Mik: That's the pathetic part of it. Unfortunately, the fool of an Act says "compassing the death of the Heir Apparent". There's not a word about a mistake—

Ko, Pooh, and Pitti: No!

Mik: Or not knowing—

Ko: No!

Mik: Or having no notion—

Pitti: No!

Mik: Or not being there—

Pooh: No!

Mik: There should be, of course—

Ko, Pooh, and Pitti: Yes!

Mik: But there isn't.

Ko, Pooh, and Pitti: Oh!

Mik: That's the slovenly way in which these Acts are always drawn. However, cheer up, it'll be all right. I'll have it altered next session. Now, let's see about your execution— will after luncheon suit you? Can you wait till then?

Ko, Pooh, and Pitti: Oh, yes— we can wait till then!

Mik: Then we'll make it after luncheon.

Pooh: I don't want any lunch.

Mik: I'm really very sorry for you all, but it's an unjust world, and virtue is triumphant only in theatrical performances.

No. 19. "See how the Fates their gifts allot"

Glee

Mikado, Pitti-Sing, Pooh-Bah, Ko-Ko, and Katisha

Pitti-Sing
Is B more worthy?
Yet
Katisha
rall.
a tempo
I should say He's worth a great deal more than A. Yet
Pooh-Bah
Is B more worthy?
Yet
Ko-Ko
Is B more worthy?
Yet
Yet
rall.
a tempo
A is hap-py! Oh, so hap-py! Laugh-ing, Ha! ha! Chaff-ing, Ha! ha!
A is hap-py! Oh, so hap-py! Laugh-ing, Ha! ha! Chaff-ing, Ha! ha!
A is hap-py! Oh, so hap-py! Laugh-ing, Ha! ha! Chaff-ing, Ha! ha!
A is hap-py! Oh, so hap-py! Laugh-ing, Ha! ha! Chaff-ing, Ha! ha!
A is hap-py! Oh, so hap-py! Laugh-ing, Ha! ha! Chaff-ing, Ha! ha!

Nec-tar quaff-ing, Ha! ha! ha! Ev - er joy - ous, ev - er_ gay,

Nec-tar quaff-ing, Ha! ha! ha! Ev - er joy - ous, ev - er_ gay,

Nec-tar quaff-ing, Ha! ha! ha! Ev - er joy - ous, ev - er gay,

Nec-tar quaff-ing, Ha! ha! ha! Ev - er joy - ous, ev - er gay,

Nec-tar quaff-ing, Ha! ha! ha! Ev - er joy - ous, ev - er gay,

Hap - py, un - de - serv - ing A!_ Ev - er joy - ous, ev - er_ gay,

Hap - py, un - de - serv - ing A!_ Ev - er joy - ous, ev - er_ gay,

Hap - py, un - de - serv - ing A!_ Ev - er joy - ous, ev - er gay,

Hap - py, un - de - serv - ing A!_ Ev - er joy - ous, ev - er gay,

Hap - py, un - de - serv - ing A!_ Ev - er joy - ous, ev - er gay,

p
rall.
a tempo
Hap-py, un - de-serv-ing A!
If I were For-tune—which I'm not—
B should en-joy A's hap-py lot, And A should die in mis - er - ie— That
f a tempo

is, as-sum-ing I am B.
Katisha
But should A per-ish?
That should he, (Of
is, as-sum-ing I am B.
That should he, (Of
is, as-sum-ing I am B.
That should he, (Of
Mikado
But should A per-ish?
rall.
a tempo
course, as-sum-ing I am B). B should be hap-py! Oh, so hap-py!
B should be hap-py! Oh, so hap-py!
course, as-sum-ing I am B). B should be hap-py! Oh, so hap-py!
course, as-sum-ing I am B). B should be hap-py! Oh, so hap-py!
B should be hap-py! Oh, so hap-py!

Laugh-ing, Ha! ha! Chaff-ing, Ha! ha! Nec-tar quaff-ing, Ha! ha! ha!

Laugh-ing, Ha! ha! Chaff-ing, Ha! ha! Nec-tar quaff-ing, Ha! ha! ha!

Laugh-ing, Ha! ha! Chaff-ing, Ha! ha! Nec-tar quaff-ing, Ha! ha! ha!

Laugh-ing, Ha! ha! Chaff-ing, Ha! ha! Nec-tar quaff-ing, Ha! ha! ha!

Laugh-ing, Ha! ha! Chaff-ing, Ha! ha! Nec-tar quaff-ing, Ha! ha! ha!

f p

But__ con-demned to die__ is__ he,__ Wretch-ed, mer-i-

But con-demned to die__ is__ he,__ Wretch-ed, mer-i-

But con-demned to die is he, Wretch-ed, mer-i-

But con-demned to die is he, Wretch-ed, mer-i-

But con-demned to die is he, Wretch-ed, mer-i-

(Exeunt Mikado and Katisha.)

Ko: Well, a nice mess you've got us into, with your nodding head and the deference due to a man of pedigree!

Pooh: Merely corroborative detail, intended to give artistic verisimilitude to an otherwise bald and unconvincing narrative.

Pitti: Corroborative detail indeed! Corroborative fiddlestick!

Ko: And you're just as bad as he is with your cock-and-a-bull stories about catching his eye and his whistling an air. But that's so like you! You must put in your oar!

Pooh: But how about your big right arm?

Pitti: Yes, and your snickersnee!

Ko: Well, well, never mind that now. There's only one thing to be done. Nanki-Poo hasn't started yet—he must come to life again at once. *(Enter Nanki-Poo and Yum-Yum, prepared for journey.)* Here he comes. Here, Nanki-Poo, I've good news for you—you're reprieved.

Nanki: Oh, but it's too late. I'm a dead man, and I'm off for my honeymoon.

Ko: Nonsense! A terrible thing has just happened. It seems you're the son of the Mikado.

Nanki: Yes, but that happened some time ago.

Ko: Is this a time for airy persiflage? Your father is here, and with Katisha!

Nanki: My father! And with Katisha!

Ko: Yes, he wants you particularly.

Pooh: So does she.

Yum: Oh, but he's married now.

Ko: But, bless my heart! what has that to do with it?

Nanki: Katisha claims me in marriage, but I can't marry her because I'm married already—consequently she will insist on my execution; and if I'm executed, my wife will have to be buried alive.

Yum: You see our difficulty.

Ko: Yes. I don't know what's to be done.

Nanki: There's one chance for you. If you could persuade Katisha to marry you, she would have no further claim on me, and in that case I could come to life without any fear of being put to death.

Ko: I marry Katisha!

Yum: I really think it's the only course.

Ko: But, my good girl, have you seen her? She's something appalling!

Pitti: Ah! that's only her face. She has a left elbow which people come miles to see!

Pooh: I am told that her right heel is much admired by connoisseurs.

Ko: My good sir, I decline to pin my heart upon any lady's right heel.

Nanki: It comes to this: while Katisha is single, I prefer to be a disembodied spirit. When Katisha is married, existence will be as welcome as the flowers in spring.

No. 20. "The flowers that bloom in the spring"

Song

Nanki-Poo, Ko-Ko, Yum-Yum, Pitti-Sing, and Pooh-Bah

sing, Tra la, We wel-come the hope that they bring, Tra la, Of a
sum-mer of ro-ses and wine, Of a sum-mer of ro-ses and
wine. And that's what we mean when we say that a thing Is
rall.
a tempo
wel-come as flow-ers that bloom in the spring, Tra la la la la, Tra la la la la, The
rall.
a tempo

Yum-Yum
Tra la la la la,—Tra la la la la,—
Pitti-Sing
Tra la la la la, Tra la la la la,
flow-ers that bloom in the spring. Tra la la la la, Tra la la la la,
Pooh-Bah
Tra la la la la, Tra la la la la,
f

Tra la la la la la!
Tra la la la la la!
Tra la la la la la!
Tra la la la la la!
f

Ko-Ko
The flow - ers that bloom in the
spring, Tra la, Have noth - ing to do with the case. I've
got to take un - der my wing, Tra la, A most un-at-trac - tive old
thing, Tra la, With a car - i - ca-ture of a face, With a

rall.

car - i - ca-ture of a face. And that's what I mean when I

rall.

a tempo

say, or I sing, "Oh, both-er the flow-ers that bloom in the spring", Tra

a tempo

f

Tra

f

Tra

f

Tra

la la la la,— Tra la la la la,— "Oh, both-er the flow-ers of spring!"

f

Tra

f

la la la la, Tra la la la la, Tra la la la la la!
la la la la, Tra la la la la, Tra la la la la la!
la la la la, Tra la la la la, Tra la la la la la!
Tra la la la la la!
la la la la, Tra la la la la, Tra la la la la la!
f
(Dance and exeunt Nanki-Poo, Yum-Yum, Pooh-Bah, Pitti-Sing, and Ko-Ko.)
Attacca
(Enter Katisha.)

No. 21. "Alone, and yet alive!"

Recitative and Song

Katisha

My doom, to wait!
my pun-ish-ment, to live!
Andante moderato ♩ = 84
p
Hearts do not break! They sting and ache For
old _ love's sake, But do not die,
Tho' with each breath They
long for death, As wit - ness-eth The liv-ing I,
The liv-ing I. ___

Oh, liv - ing I! Come, tell_ me_ why, When
p
hope is gone, Dost thou stay on?___ Why lin-ger here, Where
cresc.
all is drear? Oh, liv - ing I! Come, tell_ me_
tremolo
cresc.
why, When hope_ is gone, Dost thou stay on? May not a cheat-ed maid-en
f

Ko: *(entering and approaching her timidly)* Katisha!

Kat: The miscreant who robbed me of my love! But vengeance pursues—they are heating the cauldron!

Ko: Katisha—behold a suppliant at your feet! Katisha—mercy!

Kat: Mercy? Had you mercy on him? See here, you! You have slain my love. He did not love *me*, but he would have loved me in time. I am an acquired taste—only the educated palate can appreciate *me*. I was educating *his* palate when he left me. Well, he is dead, and where shall I find another? It takes years to train a man to love me. Am I to go through the weary round again, and, at the same time, implore mercy for you who robbed me of my prey—I mean my pupil—just as his education was on the point of completion? Oh, where shall I find another?

Ko: *(suddenly, and with great vehemence)* Here!—Here!

Kat: What! ! !

Ko: *(with intense passion)* Katisha, for years I have loved you with a white-hot passion that is slowly but surely consuming my very vitals! Ah, shrink not from me! If there is aught of woman's mercy in your heart, turn not away from a love-sick suppliant whose every fibre thrills at your tiniest touch! True it is that, under a poor mask of disgust, I have endeavoured to conceal a passion whose inner fires are broiling the soul within me. But the fire will not be smothered—it defies all attempts at extinction, and, breaking forth, all the more eagerly for its long restraint, it declares itself in words that will not be weighed—that cannot be schooled—that should not be too severely criticised. Katisha, I dare not hope for your love—but I will not live without it! Darling!

Kat: You, whose hands still reek with the blood of my betrothed, dare to address words of passion to the woman you have so foully wronged!

Ko: I do—accept my love, or I perish on the spot!

Kat: Go to! Who knows so well as I that no one ever yet died of a broken heart!

Ko: You know not what you say. Listen!

No. 22. "Willow, tit-willow"

Song

Ko-Ko

bird- ie?" I cried, "Or a rath- er tough worm in your lit- tle in- side?" With a
shake of his poor lit- tle head he re-plied, "Oh, wil- low, tit- wil- low, tit-
wil- low!" 2. He slapped at his chest, as he
sat on that bough, Sing-ing, "Wil-low, tit- wil- low, tit - wil- low!" And a
p

cold per-spi - ra-tion be-span-gled his brow, Oh, wil-low, tit-wil-low, tit -
wil-low! He sobbed and he sighed, and a gur-gle he gave, Then he
plunged him-self in - to the bil-low-y wave, And an ech-o a-rose from the
su-i-cide's grave—"Oh, wil-low, tit-wil-low, tit-wil-low!"

3. Now I feel just as sure as I'm sure that my name Is-n't
Wil-low, tit-wil-low, tit - wil-low, That 'twas blight-ed af-fec-tion that
made him ex-claim, "Oh, wil-low, tit-wil-low, tit - wil-low!" And if
you re-main cal - lous and ob - du - rate, I Shall
p

per-ish as he did, and you will know why, Though I prob-a-bly shall not ex-

(During this song Katisha has been greatly affected, and at the end is almost in tears.)

Kat: *(whimpering)* Did he really die of love?

Ko: He really did.

Kat: All on account of a cruel little hen?

Ko: Yes.

Kat: Poor little chap!

Ko: It's an affecting tale, and quite true. I knew the bird intimately.

Kat: Did you? He must have been very fond of her!

Ko: His devotion was something extraordinary.

Kat: *(still whimpering)* Poor little chap! And— and if I refuse you, will you go and do the same?

Ko: At once.

Kat: No, no— you mustn't! Anything but that! *(Falls on his breast.)* Oh, I'm a silly little goose!

Ko: *(making a wry face)* You are!

Kat: And you won't hate me because I'm just a little teeny weeny wee bit bloodthirsty, will you?

Ko: Hate you? Oh, Katisha! is there not beauty even in bloodthirstiness?

Kat: My idea exactly.

No. 23. "There is beauty in the bellow of the blast"

Duet

Katisha and Ko-Ko

Con - go or the Ni - ger, And es - pe - cial - ly when lash - ing of his
Katisha
tail. Vol - ca - noes have a splen-dour that is grim, And
earthquakes on-ly ter-ri-fy the dolts, But to him who's sci-en-tif-ic There is
meno mosso
Ko-Ko
noth-ing that's ter-rif-ic In the fall-ing of a flight of thun-der-bolts. Yes, in
f
p
meno mosso
sf

rall.
spite of all my meek-ness, If I have a lit - tle weak - ness, It's a
p
Both
a tempo
pas sion for a flight of thun-der - bolts. If that is so, Sing
rall.
p a tempo
der - ry down der - ry! It's ev - i - dent, ver - y, Our tastes are one. A -
way we'll go, And mer-ri - ly mar-ry, Nor tar-di - ly tar - ry Till day is done.
f

tr
tr
tr
tr
Ko-Ko
There is
p
beau-ty in ex-treme old_ age- Do you fan-cy you are eld-er-ly e-
nough? In-for-ma-tion I'm re-quest-ing On a sub-ject in-ter-est-ing: Is a

Katisha

maid-en all the bet-ter when she's tough? Through-out this wide do-min-ion It's the

gen-er-al o-pin-ion That she'll last a good deal long-er when she's tough.

Ko-Ko

Are you

f

old e-nough to mar-ry, do you think? Won't you wait un-til you're eight-y in the

p

shade? There's a fas-ci-na-tion fran-tic In a ru-in that's ro-man-tic; Do you

Katisha
think you are suf-fi-cient-ly de-cayed? To the mat-ter that you men-tion I have
giv - en some at - ten - tion, And I think I am suf - fi - cient - ly de -
rall.
rall.
Both
a tempo
cayed. If that is so, Sing der - ry down der - ry! It's
p a tempo
ev - i - dent, ver - y, Our tastes are one. A - way we'll go, And

f
mer-ri-ly mar-ry, Nor tar-di-ly tar-ry Till day is done. If
tr
f
that is so, Sing der-ry down der-ry! It's ev-i-dent, ver-y, Our
tastes are one. A-way we'll go, And mer-ri-ly mar-ry, Nor
tar-di-ly tar-ry Till day is done. Sing der-ry down der-ry! We'll

(Flourish. Enter the Mikado, attended by Pish-Tush and Court.)

Mik: Now then, we've had a capital lunch, and we're quite ready. Have all the painful preparations been made?

Pish: Your Majesty, all is prepared.

Mik: Then produce the unfortunate gentleman and his two well-meaning but misguided accomplices.

(Enter Katisha, Ko-Ko, Pitti-Sing, and Pooh-Bah. They throw themselves at the Mikado's feet.)

Kat: Mercy! Mercy for Ko-Ko! Mercy for Pitti-Sing! Mercy even for Pooh-Bah!

Mik: I beg your pardon, I don't think I quite caught that remark.

Pooh: Mercy even for Pooh-Bah.

Kat: Mercy! My husband that was to have been is dead, and I have just married this miserable object.

Mik: Oh! You've not been long about it!

Ko: We were married before the Registrar.

Pooh: *I* am the Registrar.

Mik: I see. But my difficulty is that, as you have slain the Heir Apparent—

(Enter Nanki-Poo and Yum-Yum. They kneel.)

Nanki: The Heir Apparent is *not* slain.

Mik: Bless my heart, my son!

Yum: And your daughter-in-law elected!

Kat: *(seizing Ko-Ko)* Traitor, you have deceived me!

Mik: Yes, you are entitled to a little explanation, but I think he will give it better whole than in pieces.

Ko: Your Majesty, it's like this: it is true that I stated that I had killed Nanki-Poo—

Mik: Yes, with most affecting particulars.

Pooh: Merely corroborative detail intended to give artistic verisimilitude to a bald and—

Ko: *Will* you refrain from putting in your oar? *(To Mikado)* It's like this: when your Majesty says, "Let a thing be done", it's as good as done— practically, it *is* done— because your Majesty's will is law. Your Majesty says, "Kill a gentleman", and a gentleman is told off to be killed. Consequently, that gentleman is as good as dead— practically, he *is* dead— and if he is dead, why not say so?

Mik: I see. Nothing could possibly be more satisfactory!

No. 24. "For he's gone and married Yum-Yum"

Finale of Act II

Ensemble

Ko-Ko

join our ex-pres-sions of glee! On this sub-ject I pray you be

dumb— Your no-tions, though man-y, Are not worth a pen-ny, The

Dumb-dumb!

Dumb-dumb!

word for your gui-dance is "Mum"— You've a ver-y good bar-gain in me. On this

f Tutti

Mum-mum! On this

f

Mum-mum! On this

f

sub-ject we pray you be dumb– Dumb-dumb! We think you had bet-ter suc -
sub-ject we pray you be dumb– Dumb-dumb! We think you had bet-ter suc -
sub-ject we pray you be dumb– Dumb-dumb! We think you had bet-ter suc -
cumb– Cumb-cumb! You'll find there are man - y Who'll wed for a
Ko-Ko with Tenors
cumb– Cumb-cumb! You'll find there are man - y Who'll wed for a
pen - ny, Who'll wed for a pen - ny, There are lots of good
pen - ny, Who'll wed for a pen - ny, There are lots of good

fish in the sea, There are lots of good fish in the
fish in the sea, There are lots of good fish in the
sea, There's lots of good fish, good fish in the sea, There's lots of good
sea, There's lots of good fish, good fish in the sea, There's lots of good
f
fish, good fish in the sea, in the sea, in the sea, in the sea, in the
fish, good fish in the sea, in the sea, in the sea, in the sea, in the

Allegro con brio
Yum-Yum
sea!
And fair - ly
Nanki-Poo
sea!
The threat-ened cloud has passed a - way,
Allegro con brio
f dim.
p
shines the dawn-ing day;
We've years and
Nanki
What tho' the night may come too soon,
years of af - ter-noon!
Yum-Yum
Then let the throng Our joy ad -
Pitti Sing
Then let the throng Our joy ad -
Peep-Bo
Then let the throng Our joy ad -
Nanki-Poo
Then let the throng Our joy ad -
Pooh-Bah and Pish-Tush
Then let the throng Our joy ad -

vance, With laugh-ing song And mer-ry
vance, With laugh-ing song And mer-ry
vance, With laugh - ing song And mer - ry
vance, With laugh - ing song And mer - ry
vance, With laugh - ing song And mer - ry
dance, Then let the throng Our joy ad - vance, With laugh-ing song And mer- ry
dance, Then let the throng Our joy ad - vance, With laugh-ing song And mer- ry
dance, Then let the throng Our joy ad - vance, With laugh-ing song And mer- ry
dance, Then let the throng Our joy ad - vance, With laugh-ing song And mer- ry
dance, Then let the throng Our joy ad - vance, With laugh-ing song And mer- ry

dance, With laugh-ing song And mer- ry dance, With laugh - ing
dance,With laugh-ing song And mer- ry dance, With laugh - ing
dance,With laugh-ing song And mer- ry dance, With laugh - ing
dance,With laugh-ing song And mer- ry dance, With laugh - ing
dance,With laugh-ing song And mer- ry dance, With laugh - ing
cresc.
song,
song,
song,
song,
song,
Chorus
Yum-Yum
ff SOPRANOS I
With joy - ous shout, With joy-ous
Pitti-Sing, Peep-Bo
ff SOPRANOS II
With joy - ous shout,With joy-ous
Nanki-Poo
ff TENORS
With joy - ous shout,With joy-ous
Pooh-Bah, Pish-Tush
ff BASSES
With joy - ous shout,With joy-ous
ff

shout and ring - ing cheer, In - au - gu - rate, in - au - gu -
shout and ring - ing cheer, In - au - gu - rate, in - au - gu -
shout and ring - ing cheer, In - au - gu - rate, in - au - gu -
shout and ring - ing cheer, In - au - gu - rate, in - au - gu -
rate their new ca - reer! With joy - ous shout and
rate their new ca - reer! With joy - ous shout and ring-ing cheer, In - au - gu -
rate their new ca - reer! With joy - ous shout and ring-ing cheer, In - au - gu -
rate their new ca - reer! With joy - ous shout and ring-ing cheer, In - au - gu -

cheer, joy - - ous, joy - -
ring - ing cheer, With joy - ous,
rate their new ca - reer! With joy-ous shout and ring-ing cheer, In - au - gu -
rate their new ca - reer! With joy-ous shout and ring-ing cheer, In - au - gu -
rate their new ca - reer! With joy-ous shout and ring-ing cheer, In - au - gu -
- - ous
joy - ous shout! With laugh-ing song And mer - ry dance, With laugh-ing
rate their new ca - reer! With laugh-ing song And mer - ry dance, With laugh-ing
rate their new ca - reer! With song
rate their new ca - reer! With song
8